D0991794

WITHDRAWN

rao's on the grill

This book is dedicated in loving memory to Robert Ubriaco, my main man, "Bubbles." I know two things: first, he is running the pearly gates with St. Peter, and second, he was the angel watching over me while I prepared this book.

ALSO FROM RAO'S RESTAURANTS

Rao's Cookbook:
Over 100 Years of Italian Home Cooking

Rao's Recipes from the Neighborhood: Frank Pellegrino
Cooks Italian with Family and Friends

rao's on the grill

PERFECTLY SIMPLE ITALIAN RECIPES FROM MY FAMILY TO YOURS

Frank Pellegrino, Jr.

ST. MARTIN'S PRESS

NEW YORK

RAO'S ON THE GRILL. Copyright © 2012 by Frank Pellegrino, Jr. Foreword copyright © 2012 by Ron Straci. All rights reserved. Printed in the United States of America. For information, address St. Martin's Press, 175 Fifth Avenue, New York, N.Y. 10010.

www.stmartins.com
Production manager: Adriana Coada

Library of Congress Cataloging-in-Publication Data

ISBN 978-1-250-00627-1 (hardcover)
eISBN 978-0-250-01774-1 (e-book)

First Edition: May 2012

10 9 8 7 6 5 4 3 2 1

CONTENTS

grilling, barbeque, and cooking out

THESE ARE words that conjure up mouth-watering thoughts that enter our minds when we think of relaxing with family and friends.

It may seem strange to think of grilling or cooking out when we think of Rao's, a small intimate restaurant in the heart of New York City, without a patio or a terrace, but it's not strange or surprising to me.

Vincent Rao, my uncle, was an avid cook who loved to use his homemade grill outside the family restaurant. Vincent taught me how to use a grill to make mouthwatering concoctions we both loved. Always fond of a good steak, Uncle Vincent bought whole sides of beef from the local A&P. He had equipped the Saloon with a band saw to cut steaks to the thickness that was appropriate for the type of grilling he planned to do. "the Saloon" is what our family called Rao's restaurant. Rao's, which was started by my grandfather Louis Rao in 1896, is now the oldest restaurant in America that has never moved and has been continuously owned by one family.

Uncle Vincent and his brother, my uncle Louis, were the middle generation of the family that brought the restaurant through the twentieth century.

It was Uncle Vincent who made my taste buds tingle when he taught me his love for all things grilled. A steak sandwich in the wee hours of the morning on the way home from a party was a great way to end an evening. During the holidays or on pleasant summer nights, Uncle Vincent would fire up the grill, standing with his trademark cowboy hat on his head, and deliver delectable delights to all.

In July of each year during the 1940s and '50s, the streets around Rao's were closed to traffic for the religious feast of Our Lady of Mt. Carmel, lights were strung across the streets, and food and sundry stands were set up to feed and please the thousands of pilgrims who came to honor Our Lady of Mt. Carmel in the church around the corner on 115th Street. To assist the people who opened stands and sold items such as heros, zeppoles, and pizza, my uncles closed the kitchen and just sold liquid refreshments.

Uncle Vincent could not resist joining the outdoor food scene. As a very young boy I helped him conjure up delightful savory foods on his homemade grill. The grill, which was made for him by a local tradesman, was heavy-duty steel, eight-feet wide, three-feet deep, and filled with charcoal. Everything went on that grill during the feast—steaks, chops, chicken, sweetbreads, and even a few secret parts of the cow and pig! On regular grilling days, steaks and chops were the norm, but during the feast everything was fair game for the grill.

There was a small garage between the Saloon and the home my uncles shared with "Mama Jake," my grandmother, Francesca Rao. Uncle Vincent always kept his new and ever-present Cadillac there, using it for his daily trips to shop and bank. I once swapped his Cadillac for my Corvette to go on a ski trip. He loved the idea once he remembered how to shift gears on a straight stick car.

With my uncle Vincent's lessons firmly planted in my mind, I began my own love affair with outdoor grilling. It has become a family fun fest ever since. I have learned to grill everything from steaks, chops, and fish, to fennel and vegetables. It has been an adventure to experiment, as well as a refreshing and classic way to enjoy family fun. Everything savory is made even more delectable on the grill. As you will see in the following pages, some surprising items—even desserts—can be cooked on the grill. In this book you will also find some of the legendary recipes that come from the restaurant, grilled!

I think Louis and Vincent are keeping a watchful eye on us from heaven and are amazed, I am sure, at how their little Saloon has grown. It has been fun for me, Frank, Sr., and Frank, Jr. to not only keep their flame alive in the restaurants that bear their names in New York and Las Vegas, but also to keep them in our hearts every time we fire up the "Barbie."

I feel like Uncle Vincent is standing next to me and guiding me through each turn on the grill. He must be there—how else does everything turn out "just right"?

I hope you will find grilling the Rao's way as enjoyable as we do.

—RON STRACI, CO-OWNER

"Happiness is gratitude manifested in the moment...."

—FRANKIE

INTRODUCTION
my journey to the grill

WELCOME TO *Rao's On the Grill*. The inspiration for this book started for me as a child growing up in a traditional Italian American family whose forefathers emigrated from Southern Italy to East Harlem, New York, then to the south shore of Long Island. I received my invitation to work at Rao's Bar & Grill in the summer of 1982 from my father, Grand-aunt Annie, and Uncle Vincent. Little did I know how that summer would define the next thirty years of my life both personally and professionally.

My first major career accomplishment was learning how to sweep the dining-room floor after service to avoid being scolded by Annie McGuire the next day, which happened often. She had a knack for finding some leftover debris I missed in an obscure corner of the room.

In addition to sweeping the floor, I learned how to set a table, polish silverware and glasses, avoid being bit by Rip or stumbling over Jocko, the German shepherd and black Lab that kept watchful eyes over the restaurant during the day. As time progressed and my skills sharpened, I was tasked to fill guests' water glasses and remove dishes from their tables when they were through with each course, and crumb the tables meticulously with a folded napkin. (Most of the remnants fell to the floor, hence my daily scolding from McGuire.)

Eventually my experience and the lack of other candidates afforded me a promotion to a waiter, which allowed me to broaden my career even further. My responsibilities included learning about the kitchen and food preparation. I was now responsible for preparing appetizers for the guests! If I only had a dollar for every clam I have opened since then . . .

In time, I became the manager of the East Harlem restaurant. I remained part of Rao's even after opening my first restaurant in New York City, Baldoria.

I cherished the late-night family dinners prepared by my aunt Anna and special guest chefs, who were truly a part of our family. Those dinners introduced me to the nuances of our cuisine as well as other regional Italian dishes and cooking techniques. Despite Rao's being one of the toughest reservations in town, whoever walked into the restaurant or sat at our bar would be invited to have a dish of whatever was on our table. Breaking bread with others made friendships I've maintained to this day.

Other fond memories of my childhood take me back to summers with my family, particularly at the home of my grandparents, Frank and Ida Pellegrino. It was forever bustling with family and friends morning, noon, and night, seven days a week. Along with friends and family came a great deal of hospitality and food.

Imagine being a kid surrounded by great food and terrific personalities all the time: The experiences helped shape who I am today, and continue to be incorporated into my life and work as a restaurateur on a daily basis. When I find myself in one of those rare moments when I am alone, I think back to my childhood memories of a home filled with company, conversation, and food. These wonderful memories have fueled my inspiration to share many of our family's and restaurant's recipes in a fun and easy way. The goal of this book is to inspire people to get together, prepare great meals, and have fun!

LA VITA AL FRESCO

One of the wonderful things about living "la vita al fresco" is the opportunity to be outside and enjoy the weather, especially when it's warm and sunny and all is right with the world. Even when the weather is not perfect, dedicated grillers always find a way to grill. When I lived full-time in New York, I grilled in the dead of winter.

Rao's On the Grill shows you how to use your grill to its fullest to create dishes that you may never have thought of making outdoors. I want to show you how to make many of Rao's signature dishes, with the "kiss of the grill" added to their already delicious flavor profiles. Take advantage of summer produce by making pasta (and even a salad or two) on the grill. I'll even teach you how to turn your grill into an outdoor oven to make a surprising array of desserts. And, of course, I'll provide you with plenty of recipes for sizzling steaks and chops, tasty chicken, and delicious seafood.

Living in Las Vegas where the weather is temperate to hot most of the time (we have been known to have a little wind every now and then), I can cook outdoors almost every day of the year. Cooking and dining al fresco is a way of life, and I have an outdoor kitchen setup that I use as much as possible. Outdoor living areas are becoming more and more popular,

and many al fresco setups have all of the amenities of the indoor kitchen.

But you don't need a complete outdoor kitchen to use this book, just a grill. The biggest benefit to cooking outdoors, aside from the terrific flavor, is that in hot weather, you will keep the indoor kitchen cool. There are no ovens to turn on or ignited burners to heat up the room. Cooking the main course on the grill can also be a boon at a holiday meal because it frees up the inside oven for other dishes.

YOU AND YOUR GRILL

Let's not debate the qualities of a charcoal grill versus a gas grill. Both are great. No doubt about it: The charcoal grill does apply more smoky flavor. But you can't beat the convenience of a gas grill.

If you are purchasing a gas grill, buy one with the most bells and whistles that you can afford. When comparing brands, choose the one with the most cooking surface space and highest amount of BTUs (British Thermal Units, the measurement for heat output). To me, a side burner is a must for cooking sauces and pasta, although I often cook with skillets, pots, and pans directly on the grill grate.

A round body design is more efficient than a square one for a charcoal grill. You want a model that controls heat with vents, not a grill with a stationary cooking grate.

Keep the grill clean. Remove the cooking grate(s) every couple of months and give it a good scrubbing with hot water and a scouring pad. Or, if you have the time, use oven cleaner to remove the built-up grime overnight. There are cleaning products for the interior of your grill, too, but hot water and a scouring pad, along with elbow grease and a hose, will suffice.

THE RIGHT UTENSILS

Over the years, I have learned countless cooking tips from my family. Perhaps the most useful is how to sauce food properly.

Too often, the sauce is poured over the main course as an afterthought. I was taught to "marry" the meat (or chicken or seafood) with the sauce. The technique is a simple one and easily applied to grilling: Cook or grill the meat until it is almost done, then add it to a simmering sauce to complete the cooking *and* infuse the meat with flavor.

I often finish pasta in the same way: Cook the pasta according to the package directions until it is almost, but not quite, al dente. Drain the pasta and add it to sauce that is simmering in a large skillet. Cook a minute or two more until al dente and let it absorb some of the sauce in the process.

To cook these dishes on the grill, you will need a skillet and a roasting pan, both entirely made from materials that will not melt when touched by flame (avoid skillets with hard plastic handles). Be sure that the skillet and roasting pan that you designate for grilling will fit on your grill. The smoky heat of a charcoal grill can discolor the metal, so you may want to keep a skillet and roasting pan just for outdoor cooking.

A large, deep skillet is great for cooking sauces for meat, poultry, and seafood main courses and for pasta. Use one with at least a 12-inch diameter and at least 2-inch-deep sides.

Use a large flameproof roasting pan, about 18 × 13 inches, for cooking larger amounts of food. For the best results, use a pan that is made of triple-ply (three layers) metal, because the bottom layer should be relatively thick to withstand direct heat from the grill without warping. For making pizza, use a metal 14-inch perforated pizza pan.

In addition to these two cooking utensils that are unique to my way of cooking al fresco, you will need the standard grilling equipment:

Long kitchen tongs, preferably spring-loaded, for turning food
A meat fork
A metal spatula
Protective gloves
A silicone brush for applying glazes
A sturdy grill brush for cleaning the grill
Metal and/or bamboo skewers

TEMPERATURE CONTROL

The heat is easy to adjust on a gas grill, which is one of the many reasons why many people prefer it to a charcoal grill, where the heat is controlled in a more low-tech manner.

The temperature of a gas grill is maintained with the twist of the thermostat. Most gas grills have a thermometer in their lid that shows the temperature at a glance, but not all of them have numerals on the dial and give a color-coded heat range. If you want an accurate temperature reading, put an oven thermometer on the cooking grate in the area where you are cooking the food.

Whether you use briquettes or hardwood

charcoal chunks is a matter of choice, but consider this: Charcoal burns hot and then drops in temperature very quickly, so it should be reserved for recipes where the food is cooked in a fast 20-minute window. Briquettes are evenly formed and formulated for longer burning.

The best way to build a fire is with a charcoal chimney. No serious grilling fan would ever use charcoal lighting fluid, which can impart a strange chemical flavor to your food. Buy a large chimney that holds at least

6 pounds of charcoal briquettes (or about 100 briquettes); some chimneys are too small.

After lighting the charcoal according to the manufacturer's directions, let the briquettes burn until they are coated with gray ash. Dump the coal out onto the charcoal grate (the smaller grate in the bottom of the grill), but do not spread them out to the edges of the grill. Leave a perimeter around the edges of the charcoal mound as a cooler cooking zone. Chicken and steaks, in particular, render fat that drips onto the coals, causing flare-ups—the bane of every backyard cook. If this happens, just move the food to the cooler zone so the fat drips around, but not onto, the coals.

To maintain the heat during longer grilling periods, add about 25 briquettes (or the equivalent of charcoal chunks) to the fire every 45 minutes or so. You can use the oven thermometer trick mentioned previously, or stick an old-fashioned deep-frying thermometer (with a metal probe and a glass dial) through the top vent in the lid.

Speaking of the vents in a charcoal grill lid, do you know what they are for? They control the oxygen flow inside the grill. Fire needs oxygen to burn. Keep the vents wide open, and the oxygen will feed the fire and keep it burning hot. For lower heat (useful for long periods of cooking), close the vents halfway. The only time the vents should be closed is when you want to cut off the heat to extinguish the flame and shut the grill down.

Keep your lid on! Cooking with the grill lid open is like baking with the oven door open—all of the heat escapes. *It is very important to keep the grill lid closed as much as possible* while you grill to trap the heat and maintain a steady temperature. I remind you to do this at the beginning of the cooking period of every recipe. If you add other ingredients or equipment to the grill, always close the grill afterward. Cooking with the lid closed also cuts down on the oxygen flow and discourages flare-ups.

You can apply the oven analogy to grilling temperatures, too. Think of your outdoor grill like an oven—you use a range of temperatures to bake, so why not do the same with your grilling? It is helpful to think about the heat level before you put the food on the grate:

High 500°–600°F
Medium-High 450°– 500°F
Medium 350°–450°F
Low 300°–350°F

ON THE GRILL

There are two main kinds of grilling: direct cooking and indirect cooking.

DIRECT COOKING means that the food is cooked directly over the heat source, be it propane flames or coals. This creates that deeply browned, crusty surface that makes your mouth water. This method is best used for food that will cook within 30 minutes or so—steaks, chops, boneless chicken breasts, and seafood.

INDIRECT COOKING means that the food is cooked away from the heat source. For a gas grill, the instruction booklet will give you some guidance on how to best set up your model for indirect cooking, based on the number of burners. In general, turn one burner off to create a cool area on the grill, and keep the other burner(s) on to provide the heat. The food is placed on the cool area of the grill and cooked by the generated heat from the heat source. Sometimes the food is cooked in a pan, so adjust the size of the indirect cooking area to fit the utensil by the number of burners you turn off.

In a charcoal grill, light the briquettes in a charcoal chimney. Dump the coals on one side of the grill, leaving the other side empty. Put the cooking grate in place. The food will be cooked on the cooler, coal-free side of the grill.

After preheating the grill—allow at least 15 minutes for a gas grill and 20 minutes for the coals in the chimney to turn gray—you are ready to cook. Always brush the cooking grate clean with the brush. Frankly, it is a better idea to get in the habit of brushing the grate clean after each use, before the cooked-on food has a chance to solidify. Oil the cooking grate thoroughly but lightly with a wad of paper towels dipped in pure olive oil or vegetable oil. When cooking seafood, be sure that the grill grate is extra-clean and more generously oiled so the food doesn't stick. The oil should not drip onto the heat source. Don't use aerosol grill spray unless you remove the grates from the grill to spray them—and that can be a hassle.

THE RIGHT INGREDIENTS

Italian cooking is renowned for making the best of simple ingredients, but that means that the ingredients have to be top-notch. Here are some of the foods that I cook with often, and some tips for choosing the best available ingredients to ensure success.

CANNED TOMATOES: For most people, fresh ripe tomatoes with a lot of flavor are only available for a few weeks every summer. Luckily, canned tomatoes are also a great ingredient, if you buy the right ones. I prefer imported Italian whole tomatoes from the San Marzano region near Mount Vesuvius near Naples. The volcanic soil gives the tomatoes a full, almost meaty, flavor and firm texture. A producer can process the San Marzano tomato variety without its actually having been grown in the region, so look carefully at the label to be sure that you are getting the real deal. The labeling should include *Pomodoro San Marzano dell'Agro Sarnese-Nocerino,* which indicates that they were grown in the Valle del Sarno region, and the Italian D.O.C. emblem, which confirms that they were grown in that specific designated and controlled area.

OLIVE OIL: Olive oil is an essential ingredient in Italian cooking, but Americans have come to understand that all olive oils aren't the same. Extra-virgin olive oil is from the first pressing of the olives, has a thick body and full flavor, and usually has a greenish cast. I use it when I want the olive flavor to be prominent. For dishes where the olive flavor should be more subdued, I use regular olive oil, produced from the second pressing of the olives. This golden-colored oil has a lighter viscosity and flavor than extra-virgin, but that doesn't necessarily mean it is a substandard product. (It used to be called "pure olive oil" until the olive oil industry felt that its name made it seem impure when compared to extra-virgin. I still call it pure olive oil.) Look around for brands you like; my favorite for both extra-virgin and regular oil is Berio.

SHRIMP: When I entertain (and cook at the restaurant), I like to use very large shrimp. They exude a feeling of abundance and make the guest feel special—and they withstand the heat of the grill without overcooking better than small shrimp.

Shrimp are sold by size; shrimp labeled "21/25 count" indicates that there are 21 to 25 shrimp per pound, and these are sometimes called "jumbo." However, depending on the region, the names do not always correspond to sizes, so it is best to buy shrimp by the number. The letter "U" in a size means "under," so U-12 indicates supersized shrimp that run under 12 shrimp to the pound.

You can buy a range of frozen shrimp in different sizes and stages of preparation (peeled and deveined, deveined but unpeeled "E-Z peel," and shell-on) at your supermarket and wholesale clubs. It is an excellent product.

SALT: I cook with coarse kosher salt because it is pure and unadulterated. Also, the large flakes make it easy for you to see how much you have added to a dish.

PARMESAN CHEESE: Your Parmesan cheese should be from the Parma region of Italy, labeled "Parmigiano-Reggiano," with the name imprinted in the rind. Otherwise, you could be buying Parmesan from Wisconsin or Argentina, which are okay, but don't have the tiny crystals of nutty flavor found in the real thing. Buy chunks of Parmigiano-Reggiano and grate the cheese yourself just before using. And let's pretend that canned grated Parmesan doesn't exist.

DRIED VERSUS FRESH HERBS AND SPICES

We use dried and fresh herbs and spices based upon availability and ease of use. We try to use fresh whenever possible, because it enhances the flavors of our ingredients in the way that only fresh products can. But that's not to say that dried herbs don't do in a pinch when certain herbs are not in season.

To store most fresh herbs, place the stems in a glass of water, like a bouquet, put a plastic bag loosely over the glass, and store in the refrigerator. Basil is very delicate and doesn't like the cold, so it is best to store it in a glass of water at room temperature. Wash, dry, and chop fresh herbs just before using, as some herbs discolor as soon as they are chopped. I prefer to tear basil into appropriately sized pieces and drop them right into the food just before serving.

Dried herbs do go stale over time, so don't buy more than you will use in a six-month period. Store them in a cool, dark place (but not the refrigerator) away from the stove, as heat makes them go stale more quickly. Before using a dried herb, rub it between your palms to release its oil and aroma.

ingredients/expert advice

When purchasing ingredients for any of these recipes, we suggest that you find a great local fishmonger and butcher to help you make your choices. It's best to talk to experts and tell them what you're preparing, because they can help you choose what will work best for your recipe. Part of the Rao's legacy is building relationships, and we encourage *you* to build relationships with the people from whom you purchase your food. Get to know them, ask them questions, and take their advice.

During our trips out to the Hamptons, we purchase most of our seafood from The Clam -man (235A North Sea Rd, Southhampton, 631.283.6669). The owner is a young man named Paul Cutter Koster, who goes by Cutter. His father was the original Clam man, and Cutter has followed in the family business. We asked him for some tips on picking fish.

For whole fish, look for red gills and clear eyes. For both whole fish and fillets, there shouldn't be a fishy smell. The texture of the fish should be firm and translucent, not sticky or slimy.

Oysters and clams are often eaten raw, so you want to be extra careful. Be sure the shellfish were harvested from clean waters. The fishmonger should be able to tell the source from the shellfish packaging. Sniff the oyster—if it smells bad, then it is bad. If they look dry, then they've been stored too long. The Clamman serves a lot of, well, clams, but buy your shellfish from places with high turnover to ensure the freshest products available.

Dominic has been the butcher at Rao's for nearly twenty years. He's been a butcher for forty-five. But being the butcher at Rao's means more than just cutting the meat in the morning and calling it a day. Dominic is on hand during dinner service, cutting meat to order as each guest comes in. He also acts as sort of souschef for Executive Chef Dino Gatto, prepping ingredients for dishes as needed. His advice on getting a good piece of meat? "If you go into a supermarket and they have a butcher, your best bet is to—I don't mean bribe the butcher—buy him a cup of coffee. He'll be pleased to make something for you," especially if he knows you.

SOME TIPS FROM DOMINIC

> Cook meats with the fat on for flavor, then trim the fat off before serving.

> Don't be afraid of different cuts, from flank and skirt steak to hanger or chicken steaks (sometimes called the underblade). With the right marinade, these cuts of meat are so flavorful and juicy.

> When it comes to slicing a flank or skirt steak, you have to cut it properly, against the grain and on a bias. "Otherwise," Dominic says, "it's like chewing bubblegum."

> Find an independent shop that deals with whole sides of beef. That way you can ask for exactly what you want. Take fillets, for example. They can come as steaks, but they can come on the bones as well. At a boutique shop, you can say, "Cut me a sirloin with the fillet on it." The sirloin with the fillet plus the bone can be really exquisite.

> To save money, always buy in bulk. Buy a big piece and the butcher will slice it for free.

GRILL MARKS:
the professional touch

When you get a steak at a fine restaurant, it is seared with attractive crosshatch marks from the hot grill grate. It is easy to accomplish this technique at home to give your grilled foods a professional look. Food that has a mostly flat surface works best to show off your efforts—steak, chop, salmon and other thick fish steaks, and boneless and skinless chicken breasts.

Be sure that the cooking grate is very hot. Lightly oil the grate. (You can simply use oil, but beef or pork fat trimmings from a steak or chop work, too. Grab the fat with long tongs and rub it against the hot grate until it renders and slicks the grate surface.) Arrange the food on the grate, positioning it at a 45-degree angle to the grate. Cover the grill and cook until the underside of the food is seared with marks, 1 to 2 minutes. Now rotate the food 90 degrees, cover, and cook to sear the food with crosshatch marks, 1 to 2 minutes more. Flip the food over and repeat. (Actually, if you don't crosshatch the second side, no one will know; one side will always be facing down on the plate.)

appetizers
and salads

SALADS ARE A MAINSTAY OF OUTDOOR EATING. THEY WHET EVERYONE'S appetite for what's to come later in the meal, and they can act as excellent side dishes to the main course. The best part is, they can easily be prepared ahead of time so that the host has more time to spend with guests. Several of these dishes are inspired by the appetizer menu of Rao's, such as Grilled Red Peppers with Pignoli and Raisins, and Grilled Seafood Salad. Now you can have Rao's outdoors.

crab cocktail in radicchio cups

Makes 4 servings Calling this light and tasty dish crab cocktail is really unfair, as it bears no resemblance to the kind that is covered in horseradish-spiked ketchup. The crabmeat filling can also be served on Belgian endive leaves for a finger-food appetizer.

1 cup jumbo lump crabmeat, picked over for cartilage and shells

5 teaspoons extra-virgin olive oil

Juice of ½ lemon

2 tablespoons mayonnaise

2 teaspoons Dijon mustard

2 tablespoons freshly cooked or thawed frozen peas

½ teaspoon finely diced celery

½ teaspoon finely diced red bell pepper

½ teaspoon pitted and finely diced black olives

Kosher salt

Freshly ground black pepper

4 large radicchio leaves

8 cherry tomatoes, halved

Chopped fresh flat-leaf parsley for garnish

1 Put the crabmeat in a large bowl and flake it well by hand. Add 1 teaspoon of the oil and the lemon juice and mix.

2 Stir in the mayonnaise and mustard, and mix again. Add the peas, celery, bell pepper, and olives and mix. Season to taste with salt and pepper. The salad can be prepared up to 4 hours ahead, covered with plastic wrap, and refrigerated.

3 Place each radicchio leaf on a plate. Fill each leaf with equal amounts of the crabmeat mixture and drizzle each with 1 teaspoon of the remaining oil. Garnish with the cherry tomato halves and sprinkle with the parsley. Serve immediately.

grilled seafood salad

Seafood Salad is one of Rao's signature dishes and difficult to improve on. But, I like the touch of smoky flavor provided by grilling. This salad should be a mainstay of your entertaining repertoire. Perfect seafood, dressed with a light and bright-tasting dressing, can't be topped for summer dining.

Makes 4 to 6 servings

1 Prepare an outdoor grill for direct cooking over medium-high heat (450°F).

2 **To make the marinade:** Whisk together the wine, olive oil, and lemon juice in a glass or stainless steel bowl. Add the shrimp and calamari and stir to coat with the marinade. Refrigerate for 15 minutes, no longer.

3 Place a lobster tail, shell side down, on a cutting board. Using a large sharp knife, split the tail lengthwise just to the shell, but do not cut all the way through. Slide a metal skewer through the tail meat on one side of the tail lengthwise—this keeps the tail from curling up when cooked. Repeat with the remaining lobster tails.

4 Brush the cooking grate clean and lightly oil the grill. Put the lobsters on the grill, shell side down. Grill, with the lid closed as much as possible, until the shells begin to turn red, about 4 minutes. Flip, cover, and grill until the lobster shells are completely red and the meat looks opaque, about 4 minutes more. Remove from the grill and let cool. Split each tail in half, remove the lobster meat, and roughly chop the meat, discarding the shells. Put the lobster meat in a large serving bowl.

5 While the lobster is cooling, remove the calamari and shrimp from the marinade; discard the marinade. Place the calamari and shrimp on the grill. Grill, with

(recipe continues)

MARINADE

½ cup dry white wine

½ cup extra-virgin olive oil

Juice of 1 lemon

6 jumbo (U-16 count) shrimp, peeled and deveined

3 calamari sacs, cleaned, head and tentacles removed

3 lobster tails, about 8 ounces each, thawed if necessary

⅓ cup jumbo lump crabmeat, shredded and picked through for cartilage and shells

¼ cup extra-virgin olive oil

1 teaspoon finely chopped red bell pepper

1 teaspoon finely chopped celery

1 teaspoon finely chopped black olives

1 teaspoon minced garlic

Juice of 2 lemons

Kosher salt

Freshly ground black pepper

1 tablespoon finely chopped fresh flat-leaf parsley

the lid closed as much as possible, until they begin to turn opaque around the edges, about 3 minutes. Flip, close the lid, and continue cooking until the calamari and shrimp are opaque, 3 to 4 minutes more. Transfer to a plate and let cool.

6 Slice the cooked calamari and shrimp, discarding tails, crosswise into ¼-inch-thick rings. Add to the lobster meat, along with the shrimp and crabmeat. Drizzle with the olive oil. Add the bell pepper, celery, olives, and garlic and mix. Pour the lemon juice over the salad and mix again. Season to taste with salt and pepper. Cover and refrigerate until chilled, at least 1 hour and up to 4 hours. Sprinkle with the parsley and serve chilled.

grilled shrimp cocktail

Makes 6 servings

For those of us who appreciate the good old-fashioned shrimp cocktail, redolent with horseradish, here is a grilled version that is guaranteed to please. Fresh horseradish really knocks this out of the ballpark. Use the biggest shrimp you can find: The big ones that weigh about 1 ounce each are my choice.

COCKTAIL SAUCE

1 cup tomato ketchup

2 tablespoons peeled and grated fresh horseradish (use the small holes on a box grater)

1 teaspoon minced garlic

Kosher salt

Freshly ground black pepper

1 cup dry white wine

½ cup extra-virgin olive oil

Juice of 1 lemon

½ teaspoon kosher salt

¼ teaspoon freshly ground black pepper

18 extra-jumbo (U-16) shrimp, peeled and deveined with the tail segment attached

Lemon wedges for garnish

1 **To make the cocktail sauce:** Whisk together the ketchup, horseradish, and garlic in a medium bowl and season to taste with salt and pepper. Cover with plastic wrap and refrigerate for at least 1 hour and up to 12 hours to marry the flavors.

2 Prepare an outdoor grill for direct cooking over medium-high heat (450°F).

3 Whisk together the wine, olive oil, lemon juice, salt, and pepper in a large glass or stainless steel bowl. Add the shrimp and marinate for 10 minutes, no longer.

4 Brush the cooking grate clean. Remove the shrimp from the marinade, discarding the marinade. Put the shrimp on the grill. Grill, with the lid closed as much as possible, until the shrimp begin to turn opaque around the edges, about 3 minutes. Flip the shrimp and cook until opaque throughout, about 3 minutes more. Remove the shrimp from the grill.

5 Spoon the cocktail sauce into six ramekins. For each serving, place 3 shrimp on a plate and serve warm with the sauce and lemon wedges.

shrimp salad
with lemon vinaigrette

Miles away from the mayonnaise-rich seafood salad you will find at many summer-time parties, this one has a fine Italian sensibility. The sweet, plump shrimp meat is set off nicely by crunchy bits of cucumber and tart cornichons (tiny cucumber pickles). With slightly larger portions, you could serve this as a main-course salad. Don't make this too far ahead of time or the vinaigrette will "pickle" the shrimp.

Makes 4 servings

1   Bring a medium saucepan of water to a boil over high heat. Add 1 tablespoon of salt and the juice of 1 lemon. Add the shrimp and cook until they turn opaque, 3 to 4 minutes. Drain and transfer to a medium bowl of ice water to chill. Peel and devein the shrimp, and chop them into ½-inch dice. Transfer to a medium bowl.

2   Add the cornichons, cucumber, fennel, and red onion and mix. Add the arugula, olive oil, and garlic and toss. Add the juice of the remaining lemon and the vinegar. Toss again and season to taste with salt and pepper. Serve immediately or cover and refrigerate for up to 1 hour, no longer.

Kosher salt

Juice of 2 lemons

1 pound jumbo (21/25 count) shrimp

6 cornichons, coarsely chopped

1 small cucumber, peeled, seeded, and chopped

½ cup coarsely chopped fennel bulb

½ cup finely chopped red onion

4 cups packed arugula leaves, well rinsed

½ cup extra-virgin olive oil

1 teaspoon minced garlic

2 teaspoons red wine vinegar

Freshly ground black pepper

tuna and cannellini bean salad

Makes
4 to 6
servings

Tuna and cannellini bean salad is a zesty alternative to the other starchy salads that you might find too often on the picnic table. A combination of fresh herbs gives the humble dish a lift, but you can only use basil, if you wish. For true Mediterranean flavor, use imported tuna in olive oil, which is available at Italian delicatessens and many supermarkets.

1 (12-ounce) can cannellini (white kidney) beans, drained and rinsed

2 (5- to 6-ounce) cans tuna in oil or water, preferably Italian tuna in olive oil, drained and flaked

¼ red onion, thinly sliced

¼ cup pure olive oil

6 cherry tomatoes, quartered

¼ teaspoon finely chopped fresh tarragon or ½ teaspoon dried tarragon

2 teaspoons finely chopped fresh sage or 1 teaspoon dried sage

1 teaspoon finely chopped fresh basil leaf or ½ teaspoon dried basil

Juice of 2 lemons

Kosher salt

Freshly ground black pepper

6 large fresh basil leaves for garnish

1 Mix the cannellini beans, tuna, red onion, olive oil, cherry tomatoes, tarragon, sage, and basil in a large bowl. Let stand for 30 minutes to allow the flavors to marry. (The salad can be made up to this point, covered, and refrigerated for up to 8 hours. Let stand at room temperature for 1 hour before proceeding.)

2 Stir in the lemon juice and season to taste with salt and pepper. Tear the basil into dime-size pieces, sprinkle over the salad, and serve.

egg and vegetable salad

Many cooks think of egg salad as a sandwich filling. At my outdoor parties, I serve it heaped in a bowl to go with the other side dishes. It's the finely diced vegetables that make this egg salad stand out. Be sure to season the salad generously with salt and pepper.

Makes 4 to 6 servings

1 **To hard-boil the eggs:** Place the eggs in a pot large enough to hold them in a single layer. Cover with cold water. Bring just to a boil over high heat. Remove from the heat and cover with the lid. Let stand for 12 minutes. Using a slotted spoon, transfer the eggs to a large bowl of ice water. Let stand until chilled. Peel and chop the eggs. Transfer to a medium bowl.

2 Add the carrot, celery, and red onion and mix well. Add the mayonnaise and fold it in with a rubber spatula. Season generously to taste with the salt and pepper. Cover with plastic wrap and refrigerate until chilled, at least 2 hours or up to 1 day.

3 Season again with salt and pepper and serve chilled.

8 large eggs
⅔ cup finely diced carrot
⅔ cup finely diced celery
⅓ cup finely diced red onion
1 cup mayonnaise
Kosher salt
Freshly ground black pepper

green bean and potato salad

An Italian-style potato salad, with firm potatoes and vinaigrette, will be a welcome change from the ordinary. Use white-skinned potatoes, which hold their shape after cooking much better than the typical baking potatoes with brown skins.

Makes 4 to 6 servings

1 Put the potatoes in a large saucepan and add enough cold water to cover. Add 1 tablespoon of salt. Bring to a boil over high heat. Reduce the heat to medium and cook just until the potatoes are tender, 12 to 15 minutes. Drain and rinse the potatoes under cold running water. Transfer to a bowl and let cool.

2 Fill the saucepan with fresh water and bring to a boil over high heat. Add a big pinch of salt and the green beans. Cook just until the beans are crisp-tender, about 4 minutes. Drain and rinse the beans under cold running water. Let cool.

3 Transfer the green beans to a large bowl. Whisk the vinegar and garlic together in a small bowl. Gradually whisk in the oil. Pour over the green beans, add the lemon juice, and toss. Add the potatoes and red onion and gently fold them into the beans. Season to taste with salt and pepper. Cover with plastic wrap and refrigerate for at least 30 minutes and up to 4 hours. Serve chilled with the lemon wedges.

3 white-skinned potatoes, peeled and cut into ½-inch cubes

Kosher salt

1 pound green (string) beans

½ teaspoon red wine vinegar

¼ teaspoon minced garlic

¼ cup pure olive oil

Juice of 1 lemon

¼ red onion, cut into thin half-moons

Freshly ground black pepper

Lemon wedges for serving

macaroni salad

Makes
6 to 8
servings

For many people, macaroni salad is a must-have for an outdoor party. It is convenient for the cook because it must be made ahead of serving in order to chill, and
everyone loves it. This one gets its unique flavor from a lot of hard-boiled eggs and
vegetables, and a generous dusting of paprika.

1 pound elbow macaroni

6 hard-boiled large eggs (see
step 1, page 7), peeled and
chopped

2/3 cup diced carrot

2/3 cup diced celery

2/3 cup drained and chopped
pitted black olives

1/3 cup minced yellow onion

1 cup mayonnaise

Kosher salt

Freshly ground black pepper

2 teaspoons sweet paprika for
garnish

1 Bring a large pot of salted water to a boil over high
heat. Add the macaroni and cook according to the
package directions until al dente. Drain and rinse
under cold running water. Transfer to a large bowl.

2 Add the eggs, carrot, celery, olives, and onion to
the bowl and mix well. Be sure the mixture is well
combined. Add the mayonnaise and fold it in with a
rubber spatula. Season with salt and pepper to taste.
Dust the top of the salad with paprika. Cover with
plastic wrap and refrigerate until chilled, at least
2 hours or up to 1 day. Serve chilled.

rao's pasta salad
with tomatoes, mozzarella, and basil

Tomatoes, mozzarella, and basil are a very solid trio, and should be used together as often as possible. Here they are, together again, in a pasta salad that will probably become your go-to version. Whenever I make it, I get terrific feedback. You might be surprised to see that there isn't any vinegar in this salad, just the tangy tomato juices.

Makes 6 to 8 servings

1 Mix together the tomatoes, olive oil, mozzarella, parsley, torn basil, red onion, oregano, salt, pepper, and garlic in a large bowl. Cover and let stand for 30 minutes. (The tomato mixture can be made and refrigerated up to 12 hours ahead.)

2 Bring a large pot of salted water to a boil over high heat. Add the pasta and cook according to the package directions until tender. Drain and rinse under cold water. Drain well.

3 Using a slotted spoon, transfer about ½ cup of the tomato mixture to a bowl to use as a topping and set aside. Add the pasta to the larger amount of the tomato mixture and mix well. Top with the reserved tomato mixture and the whole basil leaves. Serve immediately.

12 ripe plum tomatoes, cored, seeded, and diced (about 4 cups)

1 (7-ounce) ball fresh mozzarella, cut into bite-size pieces

1 cup extra-virgin olive oil

2 tablespoons finely chopped fresh flat-leaf parsley

8 large fresh basil leaves, torn into dime-size pieces

2 teaspoons diced red onion

1½ teaspoons dried oregano

1 teaspoon kosher salt

½ teaspoon freshly ground black pepper

½ teaspoon minced garlic

1 pound short pasta, such as fusilli (spirals) or farfalle (bow ties)

6 whole fresh basil leaves for garnish

tomato and red onion salad

Makes 4 to 6 servings

The best month of the year to make this salad is August, when tomatoes are truly in season and they are full of juicy flavor. To mix it up, use tomatoes with different colors, but there is something about red ripe tomatoes that says "summer."

3 large ripe tomatoes, cored and cut into wedges

1 large red onion, thinly sliced

2 teaspoons minced garlic

¾ cup extra-virgin olive oil

2 tablespoons red wine or balsamic vinegar

1 teaspoon kosher salt

¼ teaspoon freshly ground black pepper

6 large fresh basil leaves, torn into dime-size pieces

1 Using a rubber spatula, gently stir the tomatoes, onion, and garlic together in a medium bowl. Add the oil and vinegar and stir gently to coat the tomatoes.

2 Season with the salt and pepper. Add the basil to the tomato mixture. Stir again and serve.

creamy tortellini salad
with dill and walnuts

Hearty tortellini salad can really round out an al fresco menu, and this one, with unexpected flavors of sour cream, dill, and walnuts, will have everyone asking for seconds. Frozen tortellini is convenient and is sturdy enough to maintain its shape in a salad. Even if you do have a *nonna* to make handmade tortellini, fresh tortellini would be too delicate for this dish, so just use the frozen with confidence. Thanks to our sous-chef Fatimah Madyun, for this, and the other salads in this chapter.

Makes 4 to 6 servings

1 Bring a large pot of salted water to a boil over high heat. Add the tortellini and cook according to the package directions until tender. Drain and rinse under cold running water. Spread out on a rimmed baking sheet. Drizzle the tortellini with 2 tablespoons of the olive oil and toss to coat. Let cool.

2 Heat the remaining 2 tablespoons olive oil in a medium skillet over high heat. Add the onion slices and cook, stirring often, until they soften, about 3 minutes. Reduce the temperature to medium and cook, stirring often, until the onions are golden brown, about 10 minutes. Transfer the onions to a large bowl, season lightly with salt, and set aside to cool.

3 Add the sour cream, cucumber, dill, and lemon juice to the onions and mix well. Add the tortellini and walnuts and mix again. Season to taste with salt and pepper. Cover with plastic wrap and refrigerate until chilled, at least 2 hours or up to 1 day. Serve at room temperature.

1 pound frozen cheese tortellini

4 tablespoons pure olive oil

1 medium yellow onion, cut into thin half-moons

Kosher salt

2 cups sour cream

1 cup peeled, seeded, and diced cucumber

¼ cup finely chopped fresh dill

Juice of 1 lemon

1 cup toasted and coarsely chopped walnuts (see Note, page 153)

Freshly ground black pepper

summer tortellini salad

Makes
4 to 6
servings

A collection of bright summer vegetables makes this one great-looking and fine-tasting salad. With its vinaigrette dressing, it is a little more traditional than the Creamy Tortellini Salad with Dill and Walnuts on page 15, making it a good choice when you have other items on the menu that are creamy.

1½ pounds frozen cheese tortellini

2 cups pure olive oil

1 yellow onion, cut into thin half-moons

Kosher salt

½ cup apple cider vinegar

½ cup finely chopped fresh flat-leaf parsley

Freshly ground black pepper

1 pint cherry tomatoes, quartered

1 medium cucumber, peeled, seeded, and diced

1 red bell pepper, cored, seeded, and diced

1 yellow bell pepper, cored, seeded, and diced

1 Bring a large pot of salted water to a boil over high heat. Add the tortellini and cook according to the package directions until tender. Drain and rinse under cold running water. Spread out on a rimmed baking sheet. Drizzle the tortellini with 2 tablespoons of the olive oil and toss. Let cool.

2 Heat 2 tablespoons of the olive oil in a medium skillet over high heat. Add the onion slices and cook, stirring often, until they begin to soften, about 3 minutes. Reduce the temperature to medium and cook, stirring often, until the onions are golden brown, about 10 minutes. Transfer the onions to a large bowl, season lightly with salt, and let cool.

3 Pour the vinegar into a medium bowl. Whisk in the remaining 1¾ cups olive oil. Add the parsley and whisk until combined. Season the vinaigrette with salt and pepper to taste and set aside.

4 Add the tortellini to the bowl with the onions. Add the cherry tomatoes, cucumber, and the red and yellow bell peppers. Add the vinaigrette and mix well. Let stand for 10 minutes. (The salad can be made up to 4 hours ahead, covered, and stored at room temperature, but reserve ½ cup of the vinaigrette. When ready to serve, add the remaining vinaigrette and season again with salt and pepper.) Remove from the refrigerator 1 hour before serving.

grilled romaine salad

Grilled salad? It may sound like an odd idea. However, romaine is a solid lettuce that holds up to the heat and is enhanced by grill marks. Give this a try and be prepared for it to be the subject of conversation.

Makes 4 servings

1 Prepare an outdoor grill for direct cooking over medium-high heat (450°F).

2 **To make the vinaigrette:** Whisk together the vinegar, garlic, salt, and pepper in a small bowl. Whisk in the oil and set aside.

3 Brush the lettuce, tomatoes, and scallions all over with olive oil. Season liberally with salt and pepper.

4 Brush the cooking grate clean. First put the tomatoes on the grill, cut-side down. Grill, with the lid closed as much as possible, until the edges begin to char, about 4 minutes. Flip the tomatoes and move them to a cooler edge of the grill not directly over the heat source.

5 Add the romaine lettuce, cut-side down, and the scallions, perpendicular to the grate, to the grill. (Keep the scallions close together so they are easy to roll in a unit on the grill when it comes time to turn them.) Cover and cook, turning occasionally, until the lettuce and scallions are charred with brown marks, about 4 minutes.

6 Remove the vegetables from the grill and transfer to a chopping board. Coarsely chop the lettuce and scallions and put them in a large bowl. Chop the tomato into chunks and add them to the bowl along with the vinaigrette. Toss and serve warm.

RED WINE VINAIGRETTE

2 tablespoons red wine vinegar

1 teaspoon minced garlic

½ teaspoon kosher salt

¼ teaspoon freshly ground black pepper

½ cup extra-virgin olive oil

2 hearts romaine lettuce, split in half lengthwise, but still connected at the root end

3 ripe plum or beefsteak tomatoes, cut in half lengthwise

8 scallions, root ends trimmed

Extra-virgin olive oil

Kosher salt

Freshly ground black pepper

grilled red peppers
with pignoli and raisins

Makes 6 servings

It is not unheard of for customers to order nothing but these peppers. These people know a good thing when they see it. The sweet, savory, and smoky peppers are great on their own, heaped on some crusty bread, served on top of a burger, or as part of an antipasto platter.

6 large red bell peppers

¼ cup extra-virgin olive oil

¼ cup raisins

¼ cup pignoli (pine nuts), toasted in a skillet (see Note)

1 tablespoon minced garlic

1 tablespoon finely chopped fresh flat-leaf parsley

Kosher salt

Freshly ground black pepper

NOTE: To toast pignoli (pine nuts), heat an empty skillet over high heat. Add the pignoli and cook, stirring often, until toasted, about 1 minute. Transfer to a plate and let cool.

1. Preheat an outdoor grill for direct cooking over high heat (550°F).

2 Clean the grill grate and lightly oil the grill. Put the peppers on the grill. Grill, with the lid closed as much as possible, turning the peppers occasionally, until the skin is blackened and blistered, about 12 minutes. Transfer to a heatproof bowl and cover tightly with plastic wrap (or put them in a paper bag and close the bag). Let stand to steam and cool for about 20 minutes.

3 Once the peppers have cooled, peel off the charred skins, which should come off easily. Split each pepper open and remove the seeds and ribs. Slice the peppers into ¼-inch strips.

4 Drain the pepper strips in a colander. Place a paper towel on the peppers to soak up more of the excess juices. Put the colander on a plate and refrigerate for an hour or so to chill the peppers.

5 Discard the paper towel. Combine the peppers, olive oil, raisins, pignoli, garlic, and parsley in a bowl and toss to coat the peppers well. Season to taste with salt and pepper. (The peppers can be made up to 8 hours ahead, covered with plastic wrap, and refrigerated.) Serve chilled or at room temperature.

beef

THERE'S NOTHING LIKE THE ENTICING SMELL AND SIZZLING SOUND of steak on the grill. For the best results with your steak, here are some useful tips. Use the best-grade meat you can afford. Prime is hard to find, but is the top quality, although Choice, which is what most reliable supermarkets (and some wholesale clubs) carry, is perfectly acceptable. Let the steak stand at room temperature to lose its chill while the grill heats, otherwise meat that is cooked rare could be too cool on the inside. And be sure that the grill is well heated before adding the steaks.

grilled steak pizzaiola

Makes 4 servings

A signature item in our restaurants and in our other cookbooks, creating this recipe for the grill was the next logical step. The char and smokiness imparted by the direct flame add more fantastic and deep flavor, especially when the steak is married with the rich tomato sauce. I have called for large steaks here, with the meat cut off the bone, a method that I think makes for a better dining experience.

2 (1-pound) rib-eye steaks on the bone, cut 1 inch thick

1 teaspoon kosher salt

½ teaspoon freshly ground black pepper

PIZZAIOLA SAUCE

¼ cup extra-virgin olive oil

1 red bell pepper, cored, seeded, and cut lengthwise into ½-inch strips

1 small white onion, thinly sliced

1 cup sliced white button mushrooms

1 teaspoon minced garlic

½ cup dry white wine

1 (14.5-ounce) can imported Italian plum tomatoes, preferably San Marzano, drained and crushed by hand (about 1 cup)

Pinch of dried oregano

Kosher salt

Freshly ground black pepper

1 Preheat an outdoor grill for direct cooking over high heat (550°F).

2 Season the steaks with the salt and pepper. Let stand at room temperature while preheating the grill.

3 **To make the sauce:** Place a large flameproof skillet on the cooking grate. Add the oil and let it heat until shimmering. Add the bell pepper, onion, mushrooms, and garlic and cook, stirring occasionally, until the vegetables are tender, about 6 minutes. Add the wine and bring to a boil. Stir in the tomatoes and oregano and season with salt and pepper. Return to a boil. Reduce the heat to low and simmer until slightly thickened, about 5 minutes, adding a bit more wine if the sauce gets too thick. Remove from the heat. (The sauce can be made up to 2 hours ahead.)

4 Brush the cooking grate clean and lightly oil the grate. Grill the steaks, with the lid closed as much as possible, for 1½ minutes. Rotate the steaks 90 degrees and grill for 2 minutes, just until seared with grill marks. Flip the steaks and repeat, searing for 2 minutes. Remove the steaks from the grill. They will be very rare, but will finish cooking in the sauce.

5 Put the skillet of sauce back on the grill and return it to a simmer. Add the steaks to the skillet and cook, turning occasionally in the sauce, for 3 to 4 minutes for medium-rare. An instant-read thermometer, inserted through the side of the steak to the center of the meat, should read about 125°F for medium-rare. Transfer the steaks to a carving board and let stand for 5 minutes. Remove the skillet from the heat.

6 Cut the meat from the bone, then cut across the grain into ½-inch-thick slices. Spoon the sauce onto a deep serving platter. Top with the sliced steak and serve hot.

bacon-wrapped filet mignon
with gorgonzola

Makes 4 servings

Tender filets mignons are renowned for their buttery texture, but they aren't as fully flavored as other beef cuts. For that reason, they are best matched with strong flavors, which I have done here with smoky bacon and robust Gorgonzola, as well as a garlicky seasoning.

4 (8-ounce) filets mignons, cut 1½ inches thick

1 tablespoon plus 1 teaspoon garlic powder

2 teaspoons kosher salt

1 teaspoon freshly ground black pepper

8 strips thick-sliced bacon

2 ounces Gorgonzola cheese, crumbled

1 Prepare an outdoor grill for direct cooking over medium-high heat (450°F).

2 Season the filets all over with the garlic powder, salt, and pepper. Wrap each filet around the sides with 2 slices of bacon, and tie the bacon in place with kitchen twine.

3 Brush the cooking grate clean and lightly oil the grate. Grill the filets, with the lid closed as much as possible, for 4 minutes. Flip the fillets and grill for 2 minutes. Divide the Gorgonzola equally over the tops of the filets and grill until the internal temperature reaches 125°F on an instant-read thermometer when inserted through the side of a fillet, about 2 minutes more for medium-rare. Transfer each filet to a dinner plate, let stand for 3 to 5 minutes, then serve.

grilled porterhouse
with garlic oil

Bring your favorite steak house home with this impressive steak. You'll need to special-order these extra-large steaks from the butcher. I like to serve them Italian-style, *alla taglia,* which means carved from the bone and sliced.

Makes 4 servings

1 Preheat an outdoor grill for direct grilling over high heat (500°F).

2 Mix the oil and garlic together in a small bowl. Brush the garlic oil over both sides of the steaks. Season the steaks with the salt and pepper. Let stand at room temperature while preheating the grill.

3 Brush the cooking grate clean and lightly oil the grate. Grill the steaks, with the lid closed as much as possible, for 2 minutes. Rotate the steaks 90 degrees and grill for 2 minutes more to sear with grill marks. Flip the steaks and repeat, grilling until the internal temperature reads 125°F on an instant-read thermometer when the probe is inserted through the side of a steak, about 5 minutes more for medium-rare. Transfer the steaks to a carving board. Let stand for 5 minutes.

4 Using a sharp knife, cut the meat off the bone, and discard the bone. The smaller section of meat is the fillet, and the larger section the loin. Slice the meat, across the grain, into ¼-inch-thick slices. Distribute the fillet and loin slices equally among four dinner plates, drizzle with the carving juices, and serve.

3 tablespoons pure olive oil

2 teaspoons minced garlic

2 (22-ounce) porterhouse steaks, cut 1½ inches thick

1½ teaspoons kosher salt

1 teaspoon freshly ground black pepper

rib-eye rolatini
with mozzarella, basil, and tomato

Makes 4 servings

As good as simply grilled steaks are, there are times when you want to dress them up a bit. In this recipe, thin rib-eye steaks are rolled up with tomatoes, mozzarella, and basil for an easy variation. Ask your butcher to cut the steaks for you.

4 (6-ounce) boneless rib-eye steaks, cut ¼-inch thick

7 ounces fresh mozzarella cheese, preferably *mozzarella di bufala,* thinly sliced

12 large fresh basil leaves

4 canned Italian plum tomatoes, preferably San Marzano, drained and left whole

8 small bamboo skewers, soaked in water for 1 hour, drained

1 teaspoon kosher salt

½ teaspoon freshly ground black pepper

1 Prepare an outdoor grill for direct cooking over medium-high heat (450°F).

2 For each serving, cut a sliced steak almost all the way through, like a book, on the work surface. Distribute one-fourth of the sliced mozzarella over the steak, top with 3 basil leaves, then a single tomato. Starting at a long side, roll up the steak. Spear 2 skewers through the roll, running perpendicular to the roll, to secure it. Season the outside of the rolls with the salt and pepper. Let stand at room temperature while preheating the grill.

3 Brush the cooking grate clean and lightly oil the grate. Grill the rolls, with the thickest side facing the heat, and with the lid closed as much as possible, until the undersides are seared with grill marks, about 5 minutes. Turn the rolls and cook until they feel slightly resilient when pressed with a fingertip, about 4 minutes more for medium-rare. Remove from the grill. Let stand 5 minutes. Remove the skewers and serve.

grilled rib-eye steaks
with sage sauce

Makes 4 to 6 servings

Sage is well-known as an herb seasoning for pork, but it is great with steak, too. Here it is rubbed on the steaks before grilling, and it is also featured in a vinaigrette-like sauce. If you wish, grill four smaller steaks (about 10 ounces each) for about 6 minutes for medium-rare, and serve one steak per person.

2 (16-ounce) rib-eye steaks, cut 1 inch thick

1 tablespoon pure olive oil

1½ teaspoons kosher salt

½ teaspoon freshly ground black pepper

2 teaspoons minced garlic

1 lemon, halved

2 tablespoons finely chopped fresh sage

SAGE SAUCE

¼ cup extra-virgin olive oil

1 teaspoon Dijon mustard

1 teaspoon red wine vinegar

Juice of ½ lemon

1 teaspoon finely chopped fresh sage, plus 2 large fresh sage leaves, torn into small pieces

1 teaspoon minced garlic

½ teaspoon kosher salt

½ teaspoon freshly ground black pepper

1 Prepare an outdoor grill for direct cooking over high heat (550°F).

2 Brush the steaks with the oil. Season with the salt and pepper, then rub both sides with the garlic. Let stand at room temperature while the grill is preheating.

3 **To make the sage sauce:** Combine all of the ingredients in a small jar and shake until emulsified.

4 Brush the cooking grate clean and lightly oil the grate. Place the steaks on the grate. Grill, with the lid closed as much as possible, until the undersides are seared with grill marks, about 4 minutes. Rotate the steaks 45 degrees and continue cooking until crosshatch sear marks have formed, about 4 minutes more. Flip the steaks and repeat, grilling until the steaks feel slightly resilient when pressed in the thickest part with a fingertip, about 8 minutes more for medium-rare. Transfer to a carving board.

5 Squeeze the juice of a lemon half over the steaks and sprinkle with half of the chopped sage. Turn the steaks and repeat with the remaining lemon and sage. Let stand for 5 minutes. Cut the meat off the bone and slice the meat, across the grain, into ½-inch-thick slices. Transfer the sliced steak, with the carving juices, to a serving platter. Drizzle with the sage sauce and serve.

skirt steak
with black beans and bacon

Skirt steaks cook quickly and are superflavorful. This dramatically black sauce is so hearty it almost doubles as a side dish. You might want to serve steamed rice as a side dish, and maybe the Grilled Romaine Salad on page 17.

Makes 4 to 6 servings

1 Preheat an outdoor grill for direct cooking over high heat (550°F).

2 Season the steak with the salt and pepper. Let stand at room temperature while preheating the grill.

3 To make the black bean and bacon sauce: Cook the bacon in a large flameproof skillet on the cooking grate, stirring occasionally, until crispy, about 10 minutes. Add the broth (it will splatter, so be careful), scraping up the browned bits in the skillet. Stir in the beans and garlic. Reduce the heat to low and simmer, stirring often, until the juices have thickened, about 20 minutes. Season to taste with salt and pepper. Remove from the heat.

4 Brush the cooking grate clean and lightly oil the grate. Grill the steaks, with the lid closed as much as possible, until the undersides are seared with grill marks, about 3 minutes. Flip the steaks and cook until the opposite sides are seared and the steaks have only a little resilience when pressed with a fingertip in the thickest part, about 3 minutes more for medium-rare. Transfer to a carving board and let stand for 3 minutes.

5 With the knife held at a slight angle slice the steaks, against the grain, into ¼-inch-thick slices. Spread the bean sauce on a serving platter. Top with the sliced steak and their juices. Serve hot.

2 pounds skirt steak, cut into 3 or 4 equal pieces for easier handling

1 teaspoon kosher salt

1 teaspoon freshly ground black pepper

BLACK BEAN AND BACON SAUCE

4 strips thick-sliced bacon, coarsely chopped

½ cup canned reduced-sodium chicken broth

1 (15-ounce) can black beans, drained and rinsed

2 teaspoons minced garlic

Kosher salt

Freshly ground black pepper

skirt steak
with green chiles and mushrooms

While Rao's is an Italian restaurant, our chefs in Las Vegas cannot help but be influenced by Southwestern cooking. Sautéed mushrooms are a perfect match for grilled steak, but here chiles add their heat to make this a zesty hybrid of the two cuisines. Be sure to use mild chiles. The shiny green Hatch variety, from New Mexico, is my favorite, but, if unavailable, you will find others at your market that are great stand-ins.

Makes 6 servings

1 Prepare an outdoor grill for direct cooking over high heat (550°F).

2 Season the steaks with 1 teaspoon salt and ½ teaspoon black pepper. Mix ¼ cup of the oil and 1 teaspoon of garlic in a large baking dish. Add the whole portobello caps to the dish and turn to coat with the oil. Season with 1 teaspoon salt and ½ teaspoon black pepper. Let the mushrooms and steaks stand at room temperature while making the sauté.

3 **To make the chile-mushroom sauté:** Heat the remaining ⅓ cup oil and 1 teaspoon garlic in a large flameproof skillet on the grill until the garlic softens, about 1 minute. Add the onion and cook, stirring often, until softened, about 2 minutes. Add the chiles and sliced portobellos. Cook, stirring occasionally, until the chiles are tender, about 10 minutes. Stir in the red pepper flakes. Season to taste with salt and black pepper. Remove from the heat. (The sauté can be prepared up to 2 hours ahead.)

4 Brush the cooking grate clean and lightly oil the grate. Grill the portobello caps, gills side up, with the lid closed as much as possible, until seared with

2 pounds skirt steak, cut into 3 or 4 equal pieces for easier handling

Kosher salt

Freshly ground black pepper

¼ cup plus ⅓ cup extra-virgin olive oil

2 teaspoons minced garlic

6 portobello mushroom caps, 4 left whole and 2 cut into ½-inch-wide strips

½ white onion, thinly sliced

4 long, mild green chiles, preferably Hatch, or use poblano or Anaheim, seeded, cut into ½-inch-wide strips

½ teaspoon crushed hot red pepper flakes (or less, to taste)

(recipe continues)

grill marks, about 3 minutes. Flip the caps. Add the steaks to the grill and cook, with the lid closed, until seared with grill marks, about 3 minutes. Move the mushrooms to a cooler area of the grill, such as the perimeter of a charcoal grill or the upper rack of a gas grill, gills side down, to keep them warm. Flip the steaks and grill, with the lid closed, until the steaks feel only slightly resilient when pressed with a fingertip, about 3 minutes more for medium-rare steak. Transfer the steaks to a carving board and let stand for 3 to 5 minutes.

5 Reheat the chile and mushroom sauté in the skillet on the grill. With the knife held at a slight angle, slice the steaks, against the grain, into ¼-inch-thick slices. Spread the sauté on a serving platter. Top with the sliced steak and the juices. Arrange the mushroom caps around the steak.

chef nickie's italian burger

My Las Vegas chefs are forever experimenting with new dishes. I asked our executive chef, Nicole Grimes, and chef tournant, Nick Beesley, to create the ultimate Italian burger, and I love their recipe that incorporates bell peppers, provolone cheese, and just the right amount of spice.

Makes 4

grilling burger

1 Prepare an outdoor grill for direct cooking over high heat (550°F).

2 While grill is heating, combine all of the ingredients for the burger patties in a large mixing bowl and mix well. Scoop out four 9 ounce portions of ground beef and roll each into a ball by hand, then flatten to ¾-inch in thickness.

3 Brush the cooking grate clean and lightly oil the grate. Place the burger patties on the grate. Grill, with the lid closed as much as possible, until the undersides are seared with grill marks, about 2 to 3 minutes. Rotate the patties 45 degrees and continue cooking until cross-hatch sear marks have formed, about 2 to 3 minutes more. Flip the burger patties and repeat, grilling until the burger patties are glistening with their own juice. Add 2 slices of provolone cheese to each burger and grill with the lid closed for an additional 2 minutes or until the cheese has melted. Grill for about 10 to 13 minutes for medium-rare.

4 While the burgers are cooking, lay out buns, tops, and bottoms, facing up. Place 1 piece of lettuce on the bottom bun, followed by 1 tomato slice. Once burgers have finished cooking, place on top of lettuce and tomatoes. Add 2 tablespoons of aioli sauce, top with remaining buns, and serve.

BURGER PATTIES

2½ lbs. ground beef (80/20)

3 cups roasted and diced bell peppers

1 tomato sliced into 4 circular slices, approximately ¼ inch thick

4 leaves green leaf lettuce

8 slices provolone cheese (⅛-inch thick)

3 cups grated Parmigianino cheese

2 cups water

4 tablespoons salt

1 tablespoon freshly ground black pepper

¼ cup chopped parsley

Feel free to toast your buns if you prefer.

(recipe continues)

7 egg yolks

1 quart corn oil

¼ cup lemon juice

4 tablespoons salt

3 cups roasted red pepper, blended

2 teaspoons cayenne pepper

2 tablespoons smoked paprika

roasted red pepper aioli

1 In a small mixing bowl beat egg yolks at high speed. While mixing, gently drizzle both oil and lemon juice into mixing bowl. Once the egg yolks, oil, and lemon juice have emulsified—after approximately 7 minutes—add the remaining ingredients and continue mixing for an additional 2 minutes.

2 Remove mixing bowl from mixer, cover with plastic wrap, and refrigerate for 1 to 2 hours. After topping burgers with the aioli, cover again, refrigerate, and save for later use (within two days) on salads or any type of grilled meat or fish.

pork

WHAT IS IT ABOUT PORK ON THE GRILL THAT MAKES IT SO MOUTH-watering? It's probably the added smoky flavor and the way the meat caramelizes from the heat to enhance its natural sweetness. Also, pork offers up a wide range of flavors and textures—a roast pork loin is an elegant main course that tastes quite different and is an entirely different eating experience than sticky baby back ribs.

grill-roasted pork loin
with garlic and rosemary

Makes 6 servings

Pork, garlic, and rosemary are a classic combination in Italian grilling. Practically every outdoor market in Italy has a traveling grill where slices of roast pork are served on crusty bread. (So you might want to try this as a sandwich, too.) Ask the butcher to cut the rib section off the roast and tie it back on. Serve this pork loin with a medium-bodied red wine, such as Vapolicella.

1 (4-pound) center-cut pork loin roast with bones, loin removed in one piece, and tied back onto the ribs

1½ teaspoons kosher salt

½ teaspoon freshly ground black pepper

4 (6-inch) rosemary sprigs

BASTING SAUCE

8 tablespoons (1 stick) unsalted butter

½ small onion, thinly sliced

6 garlic cloves, crushed under a knife and peeled

4 (3-inch) rosemary sprigs

¼ cup all-purpose flour

1 cup canned reduced-sodium chicken broth

½ cup dry white wine

Kosher salt

Freshly ground black pepper

1 Prepare an outdoor grill for indirect cooking over medium-high heat (450°F).

2 Untie the roast. Season the loin roast and the rib section with the salt and pepper. Arrange the rosemary sprigs all around the loin. Return the loin with the rosemary onto the rib section and tie the meat and rosemary in place with kitchen twine. Let stand at room temperature while the grill is preheating.

3 **To make the basting sauce:** Melt the butter in a small saucepan over medium heat. Add the onion, garlic, and rosemary. Remove from the heat and set aside.

4 Place the roast, rib-side down, in a roasting pan. Put the pan on the grill grate on the side away from the heat source. Roast, basting every 10 to 15 minutes with the garlic-butter mixture, until the internal temperature reaches 135°F on an instant-read thermometer, about 1¼ hours. Transfer the roast to a carving board, tent with aluminum foil, and let stand for 15 minutes before carving. (The temperature of the roast will rise about 10 degrees during this resting period.)

5 **To make the gravy:** Pour off all but 2 tablespoons of the pan juices. Cook over medium heat until the pan juices are sizzling. Whisk in the flour and let bubble until light brown, about 1 minute. Whisk in the broth and wine and bring to a boil. Reduce the heat to medium-low and simmer, whisking often, until thickened, about 3 minutes. Season to taste with salt and pepper. Pour the gravy into a sauceboat.

6 Untie the roast and discard the strings and rosemary sprigs. Cut the roast crosswise into slices. Cut the bones into individual ribs. Arrange on a platter and serve with the gravy passed on the side.

pork chops
with citrus barbecue sauce

Every cook needs a foolproof barbecue sauce for their grilled meats. This is mine. Just stir it up, and you are good to go. (You might want to make a double batch to serve with the pork, and reserve any leftover sauce for another meal.) The taste of this sweet and tangy sauce glazed on pork chops is one of the top summertime flavors. And I can't resist adding an Italian touch of a bread-crumb topping on the chops.

Makes 4 servings

1 Prepare an outdoor grill for direct cooking over medium-high heat (450°F).

2 **To make the barbecue sauce:** Mix together all of the ingredients in a small bowl.

3 Season the pork chops with the salt and pepper. Let stand at room temperature while the grill is preheating.

4 Brush the cooking grate clean and lightly oil the grate. Grill the chops, with the lid closed as much as possible, until the undersides are seared with grill marks, about 3 minutes. Flip the chops and brush the tops with some of the sauce. Grill until the opposite sides are seared, about 3 minutes. Flip the chops again and brush the tops with sauce. Grill until the undersides are glazed, about 3 minutes. Brush the chops with sauce, then flip again. Sprinkle the tops with equal amounts of the bread crumbs. Squeeze the juice from the lemon halves over the bread crumbs. Grill until the undersides are glazed and the topping is browned, 2 to 3 minutes longer. Remove from the grill. Let stand for 3 to 5 minutes and serve.

CITRUS BARBECUE SAUCE

1 cup tomato ketchup

2 tablespoons Worcestershire sauce

1 tablespoon plus 1 teaspoon orange or other citrus marmalade

2 tablespoons minced garlic

2 tablespoons freshly squeezed lemon juice

1 tablespoon plus 1 teaspoon peeled and grated fresh horseradish, or use drained prepared horseradish

1 teaspoon crushed hot red pepper flakes

4 (12-ounce) center-cut loin pork chops on the bone, cut 1½ inches thick

1 teaspoon kosher salt

½ teaspoon freshly ground black pepper

⅓ cup Italian-seasoned dried bread crumbs

1 lemon, halved

pork chops
with balsamic glaze

Makes 4 servings

Thanks to Ron Straci, my cousin and co-owner of Rao's, for this supereasy recipe that is sure to impress. It's a good way to use Rao's 8 Star Balsamic Vinaigrette—other than as a salad dressing, of course.

4 (12-ounce) center-cut pork chops, bone in, cut 1½ inches thick

1 tablespoon pure olive oil

2 teaspoons minced garlic

1 teaspoon kosher salt

½ teaspoon freshly ground black pepper

1 (6-ounce) bottle Rao's 8 Star Balsamic Vinaigrette

Chopped fresh flat-leaf parsley for serving

1 Prepare an outdoor grill for direct cooking over high heat (550°F).

2 Brush the chops with the oil. Sprinkle with the garlic and season with the salt and pepper. Let stand at room temperature while the grill is preheating.

3 Brush the cooking grate clean and lightly oil the grate. Grill the pork chops, with the lid closed as much as possible, until the undersides are seared with grill marks, about 3 minutes. Flip the chops and cook until the opposite sides are seared with grill marks, about 3 minutes more. Remove the chops from the grill. The chops will be rare, but will finish cooking in the vinaigrette.

4 Transfer the pork chops to a large skillet. Add the vinaigrette. Place the skillet on the cooking grate and bring to a simmer. Cook until the vinaigrette is slightly reduced and the chops show no sign of pink when the meat near the bone is pierced with the tip of a sharp knife, about 10 minutes. Arrange each chop on a dinner plate. Top each with an equal amount of the sauce, sprinkle with the parsley, and serve.

grill-braised baby back ribs
with white wine glaze

Here's a tip for falling-off-the-bone ribs: Braise them. Cooking in liquid tenderizes tough meat and infuses it with flavor, too. My recipe mixes up American barbecue techniques, a dry rub, with Italian sensibilities, the white wine in the braising liquid. If you wish, just before serving give the braised ribs a final grilling over medium-high heat to brown them a little more.

Makes 6 servings

1 **To make the rub:** Mix all of the ingredients in a small bowl. Season the ribs on both sides with the rub. Wrap in foil and refrigerate for at least 4 hours (or up to 24).

2 Prepare an outdoor grill for indirect cooking over medium-high heat (450°F). One area of the grill will be cooler than the other.

3 Place a large flameproof roasting pan on the hot area of the cooking grate. Add the oil and garlic. Cook, with the lid closed, until the garlic is golden brown, about 2 minutes. Using a slotted spoon, remove the garlic and set aside. Working in batches, add the ribs, meaty side down, to the pan and cook until browned, about 5 minutes. Transfer to a platter.

4 Add 1 cup of the wine to the roasting pan and bring to a boil, scraping up the browned bits on the bottom of the pan. Stir in the broth and bring to a simmer. Return the ribs to the pan and cover with foil. Cook on the cooler side of the grill until the pork is tender, about 1¼ hours. Transfer the ribs to a deep platter. (The ribs can be cooled, covered, and refrigerated for up to 8 hours.)

5 Add the crushed pineapple and the rest of the wine to the liquid in the roasting pan. Cook over high heat, stirring often, until the liquid has reduced by one-third, about 10 minutes. Season to taste with salt and pepper. Pour over the ribs and serve.

DRY RUB

2 teaspoons ground cumin

12 dried bay leaves, pulverized in a food processor or with mortar and pestle

1 tablespoon plus 1 teaspoon sugar

2 teaspoons dried oregano

2 teaspoons dried thyme

2 teaspoons crushed hot red pepper flakes

1 teaspoon kosher salt

5½ to 6 pounds baby back ribs, cut into manageable slabs

¼ cup pure olive oil

2 garlic cloves, crushed under a knife and peeled

2 cups dry white wine

2½ cups canned reduced-sodium chicken broth

1 (20-ounce) can crushed pineapple in juice, drained

Kosher salt

Freshly ground black pepper

grilled sausages
with peppers and onions

Makes 4 servings

Whenever I can't decide what to serve for dinner with friends, I fall back on this reliable sausage and peppers recipe. Everyone loves it, especially me, because it is easy, looks great, and tastes fantastic. If your market carries them, use the light green Cubanelle frying peppers, which have a little more flavor than the standard bell pepper.

PEPPERS AND ONIONS

¼ cup pure olive oil

1 garlic clove, thinly sliced

1 medium yellow onion, peeled and cut lengthwise into ½-inch-thick slices

4 Cubanelle (frying) or green bell peppers, cored, seeded, and cut lengthwise into 1-inch strips

Kosher salt

Freshly ground black pepper

8 sweet or hot Italian sausages, pricked with a fork

1 Prepare an outdoor grill for direct cooking over medium-high heat (450°F).

2 **To make the peppers and onions:** Place a large flameproof skillet on the cooking grate. Add the oil and garlic. Cook, with the lid closed as much as possible, until the garlic is golden, about 2 minutes. Add the onion and cook, stirring occasionally, until translucent, about 6 minutes. Stir in the peppers and cook, stirring occasionally, until the peppers are tender, about 10 minutes. Season the peppers with salt and pepper. Remove from the heat.

3 Meanwhile, brush the cooking grate clean and lightly oil the grate. Reduce the grill temperature to medium heat (350°F). If using a charcoal grill, the coals will have burned down to this temperature. (If you can hold your hand just above the cooking grate for 3 to 4 seconds, the temperature is correct.) Grill the sausages, with the lid closed as much as possible, occasionally turning the sausages, until they are browned and show no sign of pink when pierced with the tip of a sharp knife, about 15 minutes. Remove from the grill.

4 Return the skillet to the grill. Bury the sausages in the peppers and simmer to marry the flavors, about 5 minutes. Transfer to a platter and serve hot.

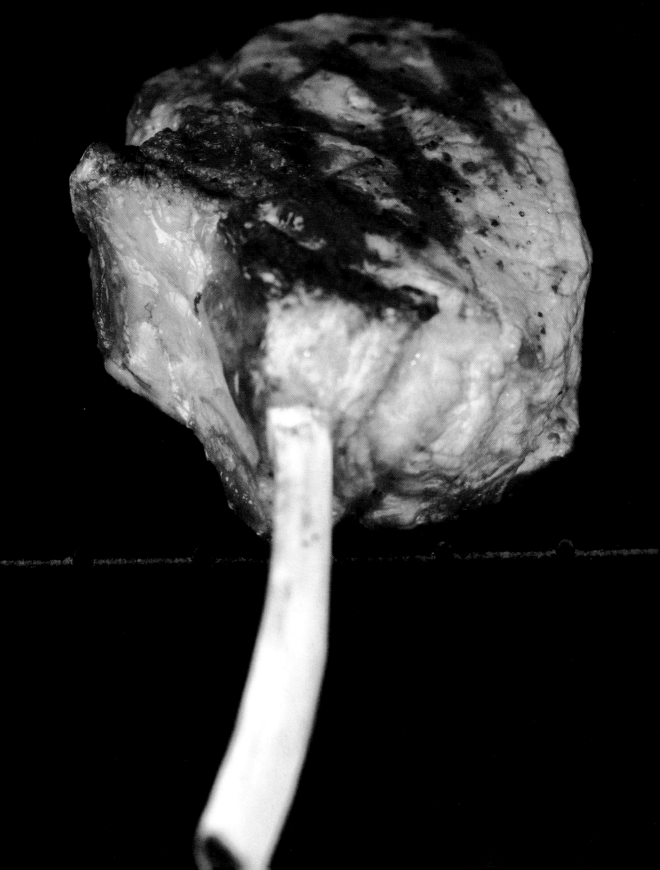

veal

WHAT WOULD ITALIAN COOKING BE LIKE WITHOUT VERSATILE VEAL?
Its delicate flavor and texture gives it the ability to pick up other flavors to make it a valuable player on the grill. Rao's veal chops with hot and sweet cherry peppers has made countless diners smile, and now you can cook it on the grill for your dinners al fresco. There is something for everyone here, from thick and meaty chops to delicate cutlets.

rao's grilled veal chops
with hot and sweet cherry peppers

Makes 4 servings

One of our most popular dishes in New York and Las Vegas, this works great on the grill. You have a generous amount of peppers here—all the better for enjoying with every bite of veal. Look for sweet and hot cherry peppers in jars in the pickle aisle at the supermarket. If you buy them from a delicatessen case, be sure to ask for a cup of the brine for the sauce.

4 (10-ounce) veal rib chops, cut about 1 inch thick

1 teaspoon kosher salt

½ teaspoon freshly ground black pepper

CHERRY PEPPER SAUCE

¼ cup pure olive oil

3 garlic cloves, crushed under a knife and peeled

1 cup pickled sweet cherry peppers, cored, halved, and seeded

1 cup pickled hot cherry peppers, cored, halved, and seeded

1 cup brine from pickled cherry peppers

1 cup dry white wine

2 tablespoons cold salted butter

Kosher salt

Freshly ground black pepper

Chopped fresh flat-leaf parsley for garnish

1 Prepare an outdoor grill for direct cooking over medium-high heat (450°F).

2 Season the chops with the salt and pepper. Let stand at room temperature while the grill is preheating.

3 **To begin the cherry pepper sauce:** Place a large flameproof skillet on the cooking grate. Add the oil and garlic. Cook, with the lid closed as much as possible, until the garlic turns golden, about 2 minutes. Add the sweet and hot peppers, brine, and wine and bring to a boil over high heat. Cook until the liquid has reduced by half, about 10 minutes. Remove from the heat. (The sauce can be made up to 2 hours ahead.)

4 Brush the cooking grate clean and lightly oil the grate. Grill the veal chops, with the lid closed as much as possible, until the undersides are grilled, about 4 minutes. Flip the chops and grill to sear the opposite sides, about 4 minutes more. Remove the veal chops from the grill. The veal will be rare, but will finish cooking in the sauce.

5 **To finish the sauce:** Return the skillet to the grill. Add the veal chops. Cook, basting the chops with the sauce, until the chops show a hint of pink when the meat at the bone is pierced with the tip of a sharp knife, about 4 minutes. Transfer each chop to a dinner

plate. Add the butter to the skillet and stir until the butter dissolves and lightly thickens the sauce. Season to taste with salt and pepper. Spoon equal amounts of the peppers with their sauce over the chops, sprinkle with parsley, and serve.

veal paillard chops
with rosemary and capers

A paillard is usually a thin, boneless cut of meat, but here the meat is left on the bone for a dramatic-looking presentation. It won't take long to pound the veal to the proper thickness. Served on a bed of arugula, this classic combination makes a terrific meal.

Makes 4 servings

1 Prepare an outdoor grill for direct cooking over medium-high heat (450°F).

2 Place each veal chop between two plastic storage bags or plastic wrap. Using a flat meat pounder or a rolling pin, pound the meaty portion of the chop, avoiding the bone, until the meat is ¼ inch thick.

3 Mix the olive oil, rosemary, and capers in a shallow baking dish. Season the veal chops with the salt and pepper. Add to the baking dish and coat on both sides with the oil mixture. Let stand at room temperature while the grill is preheating.

4 Brush the cooking grate clean and lightly oil the grate. Remove the chops from the oil mixture, letting the excess oil drip back into the dish. Grill the chops, with the lid closed as much as possible, until the undersides are seared with grill marks, about 3 minutes. Flip the chops and cook the opposite sides until the meat feels firm when pressed with a fingertip, about 3 minutes more. Remove from the grill and let stand for 5 minutes.

5 Divide the arugula among four dinner plates. Top each with a veal chop, add the lemon wedges, and serve.

4 (10-ounce) veal rib chops, cut about 1 inch thick

¼ cup extra-virgin olive oil

2 tablespoons finely chopped fresh rosemary

2 tablespoons drained, rinsed, and finely chopped capers

1 teaspoon kosher salt

½ teaspoon freshly ground black pepper

6 cups rinsed and dried arugula

Lemon wedges for serving

veal modenese alla griglia

Makes 4 servings

The area around Modena is famous for its prosciutto, which is just as mild as the prosciutto from Parma that is now available at Italian delicatessens and specialty supermarkets. Prosciutto is often used as a flavoring with delicate veal, and this pair never tasted better than in this simple grilled dish topped with Fontina cheese.

4 (6- to 8-ounce) veal cutlets, pounded ¼ inch thick, cut in half crosswise (8 pieces total)

Pure olive oil

Kosher salt

Freshly ground black pepper

1 garlic clove, minced

4 metal grilling skewers (or 4 long bamboo skewers soaked in water for 1 hour, drained)

1 large red bell pepper, cored, seeded, and cut into 8 pieces

1 small red onion, quartered lengthwise, and separated to make 8 thinner wedges

1 large portobello mushroom cap, cut into quarters

8 large white button mushrooms, stems removed

1 ripe beefsteak tomato, quartered, seeds removed with a fingertip

2 slices prosciutto, preferably prosciutto di Parma, cut crosswise into 8 equal pieces

12 tablespoons (3 ounces) shredded Fontina cheese, preferably Fontina valle d'Aosta

12 teaspoons dried plain bread crumbs

1 Preheat an outdoor grill for direct cooking over medium-high heat (450°F).

2 Brush the veal pieces with olive oil on both sides and season with ¾ teaspoon salt and ½ teaspoon pepper. Sprinkle on one side with the garlic.

3 On each skewer, spear 2 bell pepper pieces, 2 red onion wedges, 1 portobello quarter, 2 white button mushrooms, and 1 tomato quarter, alternating the vegetables on the skewer. Brush with olive oil and season to taste with salt and pepper.

4 Clean and generously oil the grate (but not so much that the oil drips onto the heat source). Grill the vegetables, with the lid closed, turning the vegetables after 3 minutes, until crisp-tender, about 6 minutes in total. Transfer to one side of the grill and reduce the heat to low. For a charcoal grill, move to the cooler edges of the grill, not directly over the coals. Add the veal to the grill. Cook over direct medium-high heat, with the lid closed, until the undersides are seared with grill marks, about 2 minutes. Flip the veal pieces. Top each with a piece of prosciutto, 1½ tablespoons of the shredded cheese, and 1 teaspoon of the bread crumbs. Cover and cook until the bread crumbs are lightly browned, about 2 minutes more. Transfer the veal and vegetables to separate platters.

5 For each serving, slide the vegetables off the skewer onto a dinner plate, and add 2 veal pieces. Serve hot.

rolled veal spiedini

Makes 4
servings

Veal cutlets are rolled up with prosciutto, Fontina, and romaine lettuce and skewered for a wonderful variation on the kebab theme. Each skewer is wrapped in aluminum foil to protect the delicate veal from overcooking on the grill. These are slightly labor-intensive, but the final result is worth the effort.

6 (6- to 8-ounce) veal cutlets, pounded ¼ inch thick, cut in halves crosswise (12 pieces total)

Pure olive oil

Kosher salt

Freshly ground black pepper

1 tablespoon finely chopped fresh rosemary

2 large romaine lettuce leaves, stems trimmed, torn into 12 pieces

12 thinly sliced white onion rounds

3 slices prosciutto, cut crosswise into 12 pieces

12 tablespoons (3 ounces) shredded Fontina cheese, preferably Fontina valle d'Aosta

1 large plum tomato, cored and cut into quarters

4 large white mushroom caps

4 metal grilling skewers (or 4 long bamboo skewers soaked in water for 1 hour, drained)

1 Prepare an outdoor grill for direct cooking over medium-high heat (450°F).

2 Brush the veal pieces on both sides with olive oil and season with 1 teaspoon salt and ½ teaspoon pepper. For each roll, place a piece of veal on the work surface, with the shorter side facing you. Sprinkle with about ¼ teaspoon of rosemary, then top with a piece of lettuce and an onion round. Add 1 piece of prosciutto and 1 tablespoon of the shredded cheese. Starting at the bottom, roll up the veal, crushing the lettuce. Repeat until you have 12 stuffed veal rolls.

3 Brush the tomato quarters and mushrooms with olive oil and season to taste with salt and pepper. For each serving, spear 3 rolls, separated by 1 tomato quarter and 1 mushroom, onto the skewers, securing the flap of the roll closed with the skewer. Brush the vegetables with oil and season with salt and pepper Loosely wrap each skewer in heavy-duty aluminum foil. Let stand at room temperature while the grill is preheating.

4 Brush the cooking grate clean and lightly oil the grate. Grill the foil-wrapped skewers, with the lid closed as much as possible, turning after 3 minutes, until the veal looks opaque (open the foil to check), about 6 minutes. Remove the skewers from the grill and discard the foil.

5 If using a gas grill, reduce the heat to medium heat (350°F). For a charcoal grill, the coals will have burned down sufficiently. Return the unwrapped skewers to the grill and cook, again with the lid closed as much as possible, turning after 2 minutes, using both tongs and a metal spatula, until the veal is seared with grill marks and feels firm when pressed with a fingertip, about 4 minutes. Remove from the grill and let stand for 3 minutes. Serve hot.

chicken

RAO'S IS FAMOUS FOR MANY DISHES, BUT IT COULD BE SAID THAT our reputation rests on two simple chicken entrées, Lemon Chicken and Chicken Scarpariello. When I first started testing recipes for this book, I was not too surprised to see how well the bold flavors of these favorites translated to the grill—but the smokiness imparted to the chicken enhanced the flavors even more than I imagined. Grilled chicken, in any form, is one of the hallmarks of a good cook, and it shows up again and again on al fresco menus, from finger-licking barbecued chicken to light chicken salad. I can speak for the popularity of these dishes from experience. An important tip: Look for small chickens at the market, around three and a half pounds each. Big chickens tend to burn on the outside before they are cooked through.

rao's grilled lemon chicken

Makes 4 servings

I do not want to mess with perfection: Uncle Vincent's Lemon Chicken has been a staple at Rao's for decades. However, allow me to say that it is even better grilled—the charred skin combined with the tart lemon juice is a match made in heaven. Lemon Chicken purists will notice the addition of balsamic vinegar to the original recipe, but the tweak is a good one. Use a small chicken if you can find one because it will cook through more evenly than one of the huge ones that you see these days.

1 (3½-pound) chicken, halved lengthwise along one side of the backbone

1 tablespoon extra-virgin olive oil

½ teaspoon kosher salt

½ teaspoon freshly ground black pepper

LEMON CHICKEN SAUCE

1¾ cups freshly squeezed lemon juice

1¼ cups extra-virgin olive oil

3 tablespoons red wine vinegar

1 tablespoon balsamic vinegar

1 tablespoon finely chopped fresh flat-leaf parsley

1½ teaspoons minced garlic

1 teaspoon dried oregano

½ teaspoon kosher salt

½ teaspoon freshly ground black pepper

Chopped fresh flat-leaf parsley for garnish

1 Preheat an outdoor grill for indirect cooking over medium-high heat (450°F).

2 Brush the chicken all over with the oil. Season with the salt and pepper. Let stand at room temperature while the grill is preheating.

3 **To make the lemon sauce:** Shake all of the ingredients well in a covered jar. Set aside at room temperature.

4 Brush the cooking grate clean and lightly oil the grate. Place the chicken, skin-side down, on the cooking grate. Cook, with the lid closed as much as possible, for 4 minutes. Reduce the grill temperature to medium heat (350°F). For a charcoal grill, move the chicken, skin-side still down, to the cooler edges of the grate not directly over the coals. Continue grilling until the skin is nicely charred, about 6 minutes more. Flip the chicken and cook until an instant-read thermometer inserted in the thickest part of the breast reads 145°F, about 12 minutes more. The chicken is undercooked at this point, but will finish cooking in the sauce. Transfer the chicken to a chopping board and let stand for 15 minutes.

5 Using a large chef's knife or a cleaver, cut each chicken half into 4 pieces totaling: 2 wings, 2 drumsticks, 2 thighs, and 2 breast halves then cut each breast half crosswise into thirds to make 6 breast pieces total.

6 Arrange the 12 chicken pieces, skin-side down, in a large skillet or flameproof roasting pan. Shake the lemon sauce mixture and pour enough into the skillet to come about ¼ inch up the sides. (The exact amount of sauce needed depends on the size of the pan. Any remaining lemon sauce can be covered and refrigerated for up to 3 days, and used as a salad dressing or marinade.) Bring to a boil over high heat. Cook for 3 minutes and turn the chicken in the sauce. Continue cooking, occasionally spooning the sauce over the chicken, until the chicken is opaque with no sign of pink when pierced with the tip of a sharp knife, about 2 minutes.

7 Transfer the chicken to a platter. Spoon the lemon sauce on top, garnish with chopped parsley, and serve hot.

rao's grilled chicken scarpariello

Makes 4 servings

This dish is what family-style cooking is all about—it's nothing fancy or even especially pretty. But, between the sweet and spicy sausage, the juicy chicken, and the tangy sauce, everyone will want seconds. You may as well make a double batch, which isn't difficult to do, since the sauce is made in a big roasting pan.

1 (3½-pound) chicken, cut into 8 serving pieces

¼ cup plus 1 tablespoon extra-virgin olive oil

½ teaspoon kosher salt

¼ teaspoon freshly ground black pepper

2 links sweet Italian sausage, pricked with a fork

2 links hot Italian sausage, pricked with a fork

2 large red bell peppers (or 1 each green and red pepper) cored, seeded, and cut into ¼-inch-wide strips

1 large yellow onion, cut into ¼-inch-thick half-moons

3 garlic cloves, crushed under a knife and peeled

½ cup drained pickled sweet cherry peppers, cored, halved crosswise, and seeded

½ cup drained pickled hot cherry peppers, cored, halved crosswise, and seeded

½ cup brine from pickled sweet cherry peppers

½ cup dry white wine

½ teaspoon dried oregano

Chopped fresh flat-leaf parsley for garnish

1 Prepare an outdoor grill for indirect cooking and direct cooking over medium-high heat (450°F).

2 Brush the chicken all over with 1 tablespoon of the oil. Season with the salt and pepper. Let stand at room temperature while the grill is preheating.

3 Brush the cooking grate clean and lightly oil the grate. Place the chicken, skin-side down, on the cooking grate. Cook, with the lid closed as much as possible, for 4 minutes. Reduce the grill temperature to medium heat (350°F). For a charcoal grill, move the chicken, skin-side still down, to the cooler edges of the grate not directly over the coals. Continue grilling until the skin is nicely charred, about 6 minutes more. Flip the chicken and add the sausages to the grate. Cook, occasionally turning the sausages but not the chicken, until the sausages are browned and an instant-read thermometer inserted in the thickest part of the breast reads 145°F, about 12 minutes more. The chicken and sausages are undercooked at this point, but will finish cooking in the sauce. Transfer the chicken and sausages to a chopping board and let stand for 15 minutes.

4 Meanwhile, place a large flameproof roasting pan on the grate over medium-high heat (450°F). For a charcoal grill, add about 25 briquettes (or the equivalent of hardwood charcoal) to the coals and let the edges gray before adding the skillet to the grate.

Add the bell peppers, onion, garlic, and the remaining ¼ cup of olive oil and stir to coat. Cook, with the lid closed as much as possible, stirring occasionally, until the vegetables begin to brown, about 8 minutes. Add the sweet and hot cherry peppers, brine, wine, and oregano.

5   Arrange the 8 chicken pieces, skin-side up, to the skillet, and add the sausages. Cook, occasionally spooning the sauce over the chicken and sausages, until an instant-read thermometer inserted in the thickest part of a breast reads 165°F, and the sauce has reduced by half, about 10 minutes. Transfer the chicken and sausage to a platter. Pour the sauce on top, sprinkle with the parsley, and serve hot.

grilled chicken
with cacciatore sauce

Grilling the chicken imparts a smokiness to the sauce that you don't get from simply roasting the chicken in the oven. White wine adds depth of flavor to round out the tomatoes and grilled vegetables for an earthy sauce that begs to be served with pasta.

Makes 4 servings

1   Preheat an outdoor grill for indirect cooking over medium-high heat (450°F). Bring a large pot of salted water to a boil over high heat on the stovetop or on the side burner of a gas grill.

2   Brush the chicken all over with 1 tablespoon of the oil. Season with the salt and pepper. Let stand at room temperature while the grill is preheating.

3   Brush the cooking grate clean and lightly oil the grate. Place the chicken, skin-side down, on the cooking grate. Cook, with the lid closed as much as possible, for 4 minutes. Reduce the grill temperature to medium heat (350°F). For a charcoal grill, move the chicken, skin-side still down, to the cooler edges of the grate not directly over the coals. Continue grilling until the skin is nicely charred, about 6 minutes more. Flip the chicken and cook until an instant-read thermometer inserted in the thickest part of the breast reads 145°F, about 12 minutes more. The chicken will be undercooked at this point, but will finish cooking in the sauce. Transfer the chicken to a chopping board and let stand while preparing the sauce.

4   Meanwhile, place a flameproof skillet on the grate over medium-high heat (450°F). For a charcoal grill, add about 25 briquettes (or the equivalent of

1 (3½-pound) chicken, halved lengthwise, backbone removed

3 tablespoons extra-virgin olive oil

½ teaspoon kosher salt

½ teaspoon freshly ground black pepper

10 ounces large cremini mushrooms, sliced

1 green bell pepper, cored, seeded, and cut into ¼-inch-wide strips

1 small yellow onion, chopped

4 garlic cloves, crushed under a knife and peeled

1 (14.5-ounce) can San Marzano peeled tomatoes, juices reserved, hand-crushed

½ cup dry white wine

1 cup thawed frozen peas

½ cup chopped fresh basil

1 pound rigatoni

(recipe continues)

hardwood charcoal) to the coals and let the edges gray before adding the skillet to the grate.

5   Heat the remaining 2 tablespoons of oil in a large skillet over medium heat. Add the mushrooms, bell pepper, onion, and garlic and cook, stirring occasionally, until lightly browned, about 10 minutes. Add the crushed tomatoes and their juices with the wine and bring to a boil. Reduce the heat to medium-low and simmer, stirring often, until slightly thickened, about 10 minutes.

6   Using a large chef's knife or a cleaver, cut each chicken half in half to quarter the chicken. Add the chicken and the juices from the board, the peas, and the basil to the sauce in the skillet. Bring to a simmer over medium heat. Reduce the heat to medium-low and simmer, occasionally turning the chicken, until the chicken shows no sign of pink, about 10 minutes.

7   After adding the chicken to the sauce, add the rigatoni to boiling salted water and cook according to the package directions until al dente. Drain well. Return the pasta to the cooking pot.

8   Transfer the chicken to a plate. Add the sauce to the pasta and toss well. Pour in a deep serving bowl, top with the chicken, and serve.

grilled chicken wings
with hot and sweet cherry peppers

The only thing that could make our veal chop with cherry peppers any better would be to eat it with your fingers to lick off every drop of the sauce. With this variation for chicken wings, you can do just that!

Makes 4 to 6 servings

1 Preheat an outdoor grill for indirect cooking over medium-high heat (450°F).

2 Brush the chicken all over with the oil. Season with the salt and pepper. Let stand at room temperature while the grill is preheating.

3 Make the cherry pepper sauce.

4 Brush the cooking grate clean and lightly oil the grate. Place the chicken wings on the grate. Grill the chicken wings, turning them occasionally, until the skin is golden brown on both sides of the wings, about 20 minutes. If there are flare-ups, reduce the heat on a gas grill, or, on a charcoal grill, move the chicken to the cooler edges of the grate not directly over the coals. Remove the chicken wings from the grill.

5 Return the pan of sauce to the grill. Add the chicken wings and cook, occasionally turning the wings in the sauce, until the chicken meat shows no sign of pink when pierced with the tip of a sharp knife, about 5 minutes.

6 Transfer the chicken wings to a platter. Add the butter to the sauce and stir until melted. Using a slotted spoon, top the chicken with the peppers, pour the sauce over all, and sprinkle with the parsley. Serve with plenty of napkins and a bowl for holding the bones.

4 pounds chicken wings

2 tablespoons extra-virgin olive oil

1 teaspoon kosher salt

½ teaspoon freshly ground black pepper

Cherry Pepper Sauce (page 48)

Chopped fresh flat-leaf parsley for garnish

grilled chicken wings
with citrus barbecue sauce

When I find a recipe I like, I stick with it. Here, I apply a thick coating of my favorite grilling glaze, a citrus barbecue sauce, to crispy chicken wings. If you want to mix it up a bit, substitute grapefruit or lime for the orange marmalade in the sauce.

4 pounds chicken wings

2 tablespoons extra-virgin olive oil

1 teaspoon kosher salt

½ teaspoon freshly ground black pepper

Citrus Barbecue Sauce (page 41)

1 Preheat an outdoor grill for indirect cooking over medium-high heat (450°F).

2 Brush the chicken all over with the oil. Season with the salt and pepper. Let stand at room temperature while the grill is preheating.

3 Make the citrus barbecue sauce.

4 Brush the cooking grate clean and lightly oil the grate. Place the chicken wings on the grate. Grill the chicken wings, turning them occasionally, until the skin is golden brown, about 20 minutes. If there are flare-ups, reduce the heat on a gas grill, or, on a charcoal grill, move the chicken to the cooler edges of the grate not directly over the coals.

5 Brush the tops of the chicken wings with some of the sauce. Cook, turning occasionally and brushing with more sauce, until the wings are glazed, 5 to 10 minutes more. Transfer the chicken wings to a platter. Serve hot, with plenty of napkins, bowls for holding the bones, and the remaining sauce passed on the side.

grilled chicken salad with dried cranberries, walnuts, and goat cheese

With a container of Rao's famous lemon chicken sauce in your fridge, you not only have ready-made vinaigrette for salads like this one, but marinade and sauce for other dishes too. So, whip up the entire batch as directed on page 58, as it keeps for a couple of weeks. The best way to prepare this much lemon juice is to use an efficient citrus juicer, such as an inexpensive electric model.

Makes 4 to 6 servings

1 Combine the chicken breasts and lemon chicken sauce in a glass or stainless steel bowl. Cover and refrigerate for 1 to 2 hours, turning the chicken in the marinade.

2 Prepare an outdoor grill for direct cooking over medium heat (400°F).

3 Brush the cooking grate clean and lightly oil the grate. Remove the chicken from the sauce, shaking off the excess sauce. Discard the sauce. Put the chicken on the grill. Grill, with the lid closed as much as possible, until the underside of the chicken is seared with grill marks, about 5 minutes. Flip the chicken, close the lid, and continue grilling until the chicken feels firm when you press it with a fingertip, about 6 minutes more. Transfer to a chopping board and let cool. Cut the chicken into bite-size pieces.

4 Combine the chicken, salad greens, walnuts, goat cheese, and dried cranberries in a large bowl. Toss with the lemon sauce and oil. Season to taste with salt and pepper. Serve immediately.

2 (6-ounce) boneless and skinless chicken breast halves

¼ cup Lemon Chicken Sauce (page 58)

SALAD

1 (5-ounce) bag mixed, baby lettuce, or spring mix salad greens

½ cup coarsely crushed walnuts

¼ cup crumbled rindless goat cheese

¼ cup dried cranberries or golden raisins

¼ cup Lemon Chicken Sauce (page 58)

2 tablespoons extra-virgin olive oil

Kosher salt

Freshly ground black pepper

grilled chicken, tomato,
and basil salad

Makes 4 servings

When you want a simple chicken salad, this is the recipe for you. It takes just a few minutes to pull together. Because lemon complements so many flavors, the grilled chicken breast halves are a good thing to have on hand to use in sandwiches or just about any other salad.

¾ cup Lemon Chicken Sauce (page 58)

4 (6-ounce) boneless, skinless chicken breast halves

4 ripe beefsteak tomatoes (2 red and 2 yellow, if you wish), seeded and cut into ½-inch dice

20 large fresh basil leaves, stacked, rolled, and thinly sliced crosswise

3 tablespoons pignoli (pine nuts), toasted (see Note, page 18)

2 tablespoons extra-virgin olive oil

Kosher salt

Freshly ground black pepper

1 Combine the chicken breasts and ½ cup of the lemon chicken sauce in a glass or stainless steel bowl. Cover and refrigerate for 1 to 2 hours, occasionally turning the chicken in the marinade.

2 Prepare an outdoor grill for direct cooking over medium-high heat (450°F).

3 Brush the cooking grate clean and lightly oil the grate. Remove the chicken from the sauce, shaking off the excess sauce. Discard the sauce. Place the chicken on the grate. Grill the chicken breast halves, with the lid closed as much as possible, until the undersides are seared with grill marks, about 5 minutes. Flip the chicken and grill until the opposite sides are seared and the chicken breast halves feel firm and resilient when pressed in the center with a fingertip, about 6 minutes. Transfer to a chopping board. Let the chicken stand for 5 minutes.

4 Meanwhile, toss the tomatoes, basil leaves, and pignoli in a large bowl with the remaining ¼ cup lemon sauce and the oil. Spread out on a serving platter. Season to taste with salt and pepper.

5 Cut the chicken breast halves crosswise, against the grain, into ½-inch-thick slices. Arrange on the tomato and basil salad and serve.

grill-roasted chicken
with garlic butter baste

I love my grill rotisserie, and I use it often, especially to make this chicken. I know that not everyone has a rotisserie, but I still wanted to share this recipe. Luckily, you get almost the same results by roasting the chicken in a pan on the grill.

Makes 4 to 6 servings

1 Prepare an outdoor grill for indirect cooking over medium heat (400°F).

2 **To make the basting mixture:** Heat the butter, oil, garlic, and rosemary together in a small saucepan over low heat until the butter melts, about 5 minutes.

3 Season the cavity of the chicken with ¼ teaspoon salt and ¼ teaspoon pepper. Stuff the lemon halves, onion, garlic, and rosemary inside the cavity. Brush the outside of the chicken with some of the basting mixture. Season with ½ teaspoon salt and ¼ teaspoon pepper. Using kitchen twine, tie the ends of the drumsticks together and tie the wings to the body.

4 Place the chicken on a roasting rack in a flameproof roasting pan. Grill the chicken, with the lid closed, basting every 20 minutes or so with the basting mixture, until an instant-read thermometer inserted in the thickest part of the thigh (not touching a bone) reads 165°F, about 1½ hours. Transfer to a chopping board.

5 Let the chicken stand for 15 minutes. Using a heavy knife and kitchen shears, cut the chicken into 2 wings, 2 drumsticks, 2 thighs, and 2 chicken breast halves; then cut each chicken breast half crosswise into 3 pieces.

6 Skim the fat from the pan juices. Return the pan to a hot area of the grill and heat until the pan juices are sizzling. Add ½ cup water and the wine and bring to a boil. Cook until reduced by half, about 2 minutes. Pour over the chicken and serve.

BASTING MIXTURE

4 tablespoons (½ stick) unsalted butter

1 tablespoon extra-virgin olive oil

4 garlic cloves, crushed under a knife and peeled

2 teaspoons chopped fresh rosemary

1 (4-pound) chicken, giblets removed

Kosher salt

Freshly ground black pepper

1 lemon, halved

1 small onion, quartered

7 unpeeled garlic cloves

4 (3-inch) sprigs rosemary

¼ cup dry white wine

seafood

MANY OF US HAVE MEMORIES OF SUMMERTIME SEASIDE VACATIONS with meals made from sparkling fresh seafood right off the boat. There is something about eating fish outside that makes it taste better—just ask anyone who's been to a clambake. I've taken a wide range of seafood dishes and cooked them on the grill. To discourage seafood sticking to the grill, be sure the grates are extra-clean and well-oiled, or to avoid the problem altogether, cook seafood or fish that is prone to stick on aluminum foil that is coated with vegetable oil spray.

grilled lobster
with garlic-oregano bread crumbs

Makes 2 servings

Whenever lobster is served, the guests know that they are in for a special treat, as it is never the least expensive item at the market. This is one of the easiest ways to cook the sweet meat of this crustacean, with a light wine sauce for dipping. Although I've made this as a dinner for two, it could be doubled to serve four guests.

HERBED BREAD CRUMBS

1 cup plain dried bread crumbs

1 tablespoon finely chopped fresh oregano

1½ teaspoons minced garlic

2 tablespoons extra-virgin olive oil

Kosher salt

Freshly ground black pepper

1 (1½-pound) lobster

¼ cup vegetable oil

3 garlic cloves, crushed under a knife and peeled

1¼ cups dry white wine

¼ cup finely chopped fresh flat-leaf parsley for serving

Lemon wedges for serving

1 Preheat an outdoor grill for (indirect) cooking over medium-high heat (450°F).

2 **To make the herbed bread crumbs:** Mix the bread crumbs, oregano, and minced garlic together in a small bowl. Stir in the olive oil to make a moist, sandy mixture. Season to taste with salt and pepper.

3 Using the tip of a large sharp knife, kill the lobster by cutting through the crease in the shell behind the head. Split the lobster in half lengthwise, and discard the head sac and intestinal vein. Crack the claws with the back side of the knife. Pat the bread crumb mixture over the exposed lobster meat.

4 Place a large flameproof roasting pan on the cooking grate. Add the oil and garlic. Cook, with the lid closed, until the garlic shimmers, about 2 minutes. Add the lobster halves, bread crumb–side up, to the pan. Cook the lobsters until the shells begin to turn red, about 5 minutes. Add the wine to the pan. Continue cooking, basting with the pan juices every 3 to 5 minutes, until the lobster meat is opaque and the crumbs are golden brown, about 8 to 12 minutes more.

5 Transfer each lobster half to a dinner plate. Sprinkle with parsley and pour equal amounts of the pan juices around the lobsters. Serve hot, with the lemon wedges.

lobster fra diavolo

Makes 4 servings

Any time you see "Fra Diavolo" on a menu, you know it is going to be as hot as the *diavolo*—I mean devil. Add the amount of hot pepper that you and your guests will like, keeping in mind that the heat is supposed to enhance the sweet lobster and not overwhelm it. The sauce is best served with pasta, but if you aren't in the mood for that, just serve the lobster and sauce with crusty bread.

2 (1½-pound) lobsters

2 tablespoons pure olive oil

4 garlic cloves, crushed under a knife and peeled

1 tablespoon finely chopped shallots

1¼ cups dry white wine

1 (28-ounce) can Italian plum tomatoes, preferably San Marzano, drained, juices reserved, and tomatoes hand-crushed

½ teaspoon crushed hot red pepper flakes, (or more or less to taste)

1 pound linguine or spaghetti

¼ cup hand-torn fresh basil leaves

Basil sprigs for garnish

1 Preheat an outdoor grill for indirect cooking over medium-high heat (450°F). Bring a large pot of lightly salted water to a boil over high heat on the stovetop or on the side burner of a gas grill.

2 Using the tip of a large sharp knife, kill each lobster by cutting through the crease in the shell behind the head. Discard the head. Cut off the small legs from each tail section and discard. Cut off the claws at the first joint, and crack the claws. Cut off the "arms" and crack them.

3 Place a large flameproof roasting pan on the cooking grate. Add the oil and garlic. Cook, with the lid closed as much as possible, until the oil shimmers, about 2 minutes. Add the lobster pieces, shell-side down. Cook, with the lid closed as much as possible, until the lobster shells begin to turn red, about 3 minutes. Stir the shallots into the oil, and let them cook until softened, about 2 minutes. Add the wine and bring to a boil. Stir in the tomatoes and their juices along with the red pepper flakes into the pan. Cook, occasionally turning the lobster in the sauce, until the lobster meat is opaque, about 10 minutes. Remove for sauce and set aside.

4 Allow sauce to cook for an additional 10 minutes, add the linguine to the boiling salted water, and cook according to the package directions until almost al dente. Drain the linguine.

5 Using tongs, add the linguine to the roasting pan and cook, stirring occasionally, until al dente and well coated with sauce, about 1 minute. Add the torn basil.

6 Divide the pasta among four serving bowls. Top with equal amounts of the lobster (remove the meat from the shell, if you wish) and garnish with the basil sprigs. Serve hot.

grilled seafood-stuffed calamari

Makes 4 servings

For countless Italian families, the Christmas Eve meal means "the feast of the seven fishes," when a parade of seafood dishes is served. This is one of the most popular floats in the parade, but it is too good to reserve for holiday cooking. I like it on the simple side, with just a squeeze of lemon, but many folks serve the calamari with their favorite tomato sauce.

STUFFING

3 large shrimp in the shell

1 thawed frozen lobster tail, split lengthwise

½ cup plain dried bread crumbs

⅓ cup jumbo lump crabmeat, picked over for cartilage and shells

1 tablespoon finely chopped red bell pepper

1 tablespoon diced celery

1 tablespoon pitted and chopped black olives, such as Gaeta

1 tablespoon minced fresh oregano

1 tablespoon minced fresh flat-leaf parsley

2 tablespoons bottled clam juice

Juice of ½ lemon

1 tablespoon dry white wine

2 tablespoons pure olive oil

Kosher salt

Freshly ground black pepper

8 calamari sacs, cleaned, heads and tentacles removed

16 wooden toothpicks, soaked in water for at least 30 minutes

Nonstick vegetable oil spray for the foil

Lemon wedges for serving

1 Prepare an outdoor grill for direct cooking over medium-high heat (450°F).

2 **To make the stuffing:** Brush the cooking grate clean and generously oil the grate. Place the shrimp and lobster on the grate. Grill, with the lid closed as much as possible, turning occasionally, until the shrimp and lobster meat turn opaque, about 5 minutes. Remove from the grill. Transfer to a chopping board and let cool. Peel and devein the shrimp and remove the lobster meat from the shell. Finely chop the shrimp and lobster meat. Transfer to a medium bowl.

3 Add the bread crumbs, crabmeat, red pepper, celery, olives, oregano, and parsley and mix well. Add the clam juice, lemon juice, wine, and oil and mix until moistened. Season to taste with salt and pepper. Fill the calamari sacs with the stuffing, making sure not to overstuff, but filling the sacs to the tips and leaving ¼ inch headroom at the open ends. Secure each sac closed with 2 toothpicks that have been soaked in water.

4 Place a large sheet of heavy-duty aluminum foil on the cooking grate. Spray with the nonstick spray. Place the calamari on the foil. Cook, with the lid closed as much as possible, until the calamari are opaque, about 15 minutes. Transfer the calamari to a platter. Discard the foil.

5 Generously oil the cooking grate. Return the calamari to the grate and cook until the undersides are seared with grill marks, about 1 minute on each side. Return the calamari to the platter and serve hot with the lemon wedges.

mussels in white wine sauce

Makes 4 servings

Dining al fresco is all about casual cooking and eating. Mussels cooked in white wine is a dish that requires eating with your fingers. It also calls for a big loaf of crusty bread for soaking up the juices. If the mussels have their "beards" attached to the shells, tug them off with a pair of pliers.

3 pounds mussels

¼ cup pure olive oil

6 garlic cloves, crushed under a knife and peeled

1 cup dry white wine

2 tablespoons chopped fresh flat-leaf parsley

Kosher salt

Freshly ground black pepper

1 Preheat an outdoor grill for direct cooking over medium-high heat (450°F).

2 Scrub the mussels well under cold running water, and discard any mussels that are gaping open or feel heavier than the other mussels. Transfer the mussels to a large bowl of salted water and let stand while the grill is preheating. Drain just before using.

3 Place a large metal roasting pan on the cooking grate. Add the oil and garlic. Cook, with the lid closed as much as possible, until the garlic begins to brown, about 1 minute. Add the mussels and wine. Cook, shaking the pan occasionally, until the mussels open, 5 to 7 minutes. Stir in the parsley. Season to taste with salt and pepper. Discard any unopened mussels.

4 Transfer the mussels and the sauce to four deep soup bowls and serve hot with crusty bread.

grilled black cod
with fennel, lemon, and wine

Let's face it: Fish fillets have a tendency to stick to grill grates. Black cod (and other oily fish, such as bluefish) is very forgiving because of its natural fat content and can be cooked more than medium-rare without fear of overcooking. This recipe takes place in two parts: cooking the fish directly on the grill, and then creating the savory, vegetable-laden sauce alongside while the fish cooks.

Makes 4 servings

1 Prepare an outdoor grill for direct cooking over medium-high heat (450°F).

2 **To make the sauce:** Place a large flameproof skillet on the cooking grate. Add the oil and garlic and cook over medium heat until the oil shimmers, about 2 minutes. Add the fennel and cook, stirring occasionally, until softened, about 3 minutes. Add the cherry tomatoes and olives and cook, stirring often, until the tomatoes have softened, about 4 minutes. Add the wine and lemon juice and bring to a boil. Remove from the heat.

3 Brush the cooking grate clean and generously oil it. Season the fish fillets with ½ teaspoon salt and ½ teaspoon pepper. Place the fillets on the grate, skin-side down. Grill, with the lid closed as much as possible, until the undersides are seared with grill marks, about 2 minutes. Flip the fish and grill until the opposite sides are seared, about 2 minutes more.

4 Return the skillet to the cooking grate. Add the fillets to the sauce. Cook until the fish is opaque when pierced in the center, about 4 minutes more. Transfer the fish to a serving platter. Remove the sauce from the heat. Whisk in the butter. Season to taste with salt and pepper. Pour the sauce over the fish. Sprinkle with the parsley and serve hot.

SAUCE

¼ cup extra-virgin olive oil

2 garlic cloves, sliced

½ fennel bulb, trimmed, cored, and thinly sliced crosswise

1 cup halved cherry tomatoes

½ cup pitted and coarsely chopped Gaeta olives

¼ cup dry white wine

Juice of 1 lemon

4 (6-ounce) black cod (also called sablefish) fillets, skin on

Kosher salt

Freshly ground black pepper

1 tablespoon unsalted butter

Chopped fresh flat-leaf parsley for garnish

grilled branzino in cartoccio

Makes 4 servings

Branzino used to be a fish variety that was only available at restaurants, but during the last few years, it has become available at well-stocked seafood stores and supermarkets. That's good news for the grilling fan, because its firm, meaty flesh is delicious. A common way of cooking branzino is in a fish basket, a tool that doesn't fit on many grills. Cooking the long whole fish in aluminum foil is a reliable and tasty method.

2 (1¼-pound) whole branzino (also called sea bass), cleaned

Kosher salt

Freshly ground black pepper

8 thin lemon slices

2 tablespoons finely chopped fresh rosemary

2 tablespoons finely chopped fresh tarragon

6 sprigs thyme

4 garlic cloves, crushed under a knife and peeled

4 tablespoons (½ stick) unsalted butter, thinly sliced

Nonstick vegetable oil spray for the foil

4 cups packed arugula leaves

Extra-virgin olive oil

Chopped fresh flat-leaf parsley for garnish

Lemon wedges for serving

1 Prepare an outdoor grill for direct cooking over medium heat (400°F).

2 For each fish, season inside and out with ½ teaspoon salt and ½ teaspoon pepper. Stuff each cavity with 4 lemon slices, 1 tablespoon of rosemary, 1 tablespoon of tarragon, 3 thyme sprigs, and 2 garlic cloves, then top with 2 tablespoons of butter. Place each fish on a large piece of heavy-duty aluminum foil that has been coated with the nonstick vegetable spray. Bring up the sides of the foil to enclose the fish, leaving the foil slightly open at the top.

3 Place the foil packets on the grill. Cook, with the lid closed as much as possible, until the fish flesh is barely opaque when pierced in the thickest part with the tip of a sharp knife, about 22 minutes. During the last 2 minutes of grilling, completely open up the foil to expose the top of the fish. Remove the fish in the foil from the grill.

4 One fish at a time, slide the branzino off the foil onto a serving platter. At the tail of the fish, use a fork to scrape up the end of the skin, making sure to catch the skin between the tines of the fork. Then, rotating the fork toward the head of fish, twirl the fish skin off the flesh. Discard the skin. Slide the fork underneath the flesh to loosen it from the backbone. Using 2 forks, lift the fillet from the bones and

transfer it to a dinner plate. Starting at the tail, lift off and discard the bone structure. Slide a fork between the bottom fillet and the skin to loosen the flesh. Transfer the flesh to a plate and cover with aluminum foil to keep warm. You should have 4 boned fillets.

5 Toss the arugula with 2 tablespoons olive oil and season to taste with salt and pepper. Divide the arugula among four dinner plates. Top each with a fish fillet. Drizzle with olive oil and sprinkle with parsley. Season with salt and pepper and serve with the lemon wedges.

grilled shrimp oreganato

The slightly spicy flavor of fresh oregano is delicious with grilled shrimp. You'll find the herb both in the basting sauce and added as a finishing touch before serving. I like to use the largest shrimp I can find for this dish because they cook longer and pick up more smokiness, but you could use smaller shrimp (up to 25 shrimp per pound), if you wish, cooked until just opaque.

Makes 4 servings

1 Prepare an outdoor grill for direct cooking over medium heat (400°F).

2 **To make the basting sauce:** Heat the oil and garlic together in a medium saucepan over medium heat until the garlic turns golden, about 3 minutes. Remove from the heat, add the oregano, and stir well. Add the butter and wine and stir until the butter is melted.

3 Season the shrimp all over with the salt and pepper. Spear 4 shrimp on each skewer. Brush well with the basting sauce.

4 Brush the cooking grate clean and generously oil the grate. Place the skewers on the grate. Grill until the undersides are seared with grill marks, about 1½ minutes. Flip and brush the tops with the basting sauce. Grill until the opposite sides are seared, about 1½ minutes. Flip, brush with the basting sauce, and sprinkle each skewer with 1 tablespoon of the bread crumbs. Grill until the crumbs begin to brown, about 2 minutes. Flip the skewers, and repeat with the basting sauce and the remaining bread crumbs. Grill, turning occasionally, until the crumbs are toasted and the shrimp are opaque, about 2 minutes more.

5 Transfer each skewer to a dinner plate. Sprinkle with oregano and serve hot with the lemon quarters.

BASTING SAUCE

¼ cup pure olive oil

3 tablespoons minced garlic

½ cup finely chopped fresh oregano

4 tablespoons (½ stick) unsalted butter, thinly sliced

¼ cup dry white wine

16 colossal (U-16) shrimp, peeled and deveined, with tail segment left attached

½ teaspoon kosher salt

½ teaspoon freshly ground black pepper

4 metal grilling skewers (or 4 long bamboo skewers soaked in water for 1 hour, drained)

4 tablespoons plain dried bread crumbs

Chopped fresh oregano for garnish

2 lemons, quartered

grilled salmon
with asparagus and almonds

Makes 4
servings

Salmon is always a good bet for grilling. Look for wild-caught, instead of farm-raised, fillets, because they have a richer flavor. Cook some asparagus on the grill at the same time—the color combination of the pink fish and green spears is a winner, and the flavor is great, too.

1 pound thin asparagus, woody stem ends snapped off

3 tablespoons pure olive oil

Kosher salt

Freshly ground black pepper

¼ cup sliced almonds

4 tablespoons (½ stick) unsalted butter

½ cup dry white wine

2 tablespoons freshly squeezed lemon juice

4 (6-ounce) salmon fillets with skin, preferably wild-caught salmon, skin on

1 Prepare an outdoor grill for direct cooking over high heat (500°F).

2 Toss the asparagus with 1 tablespoon of the oil in a large bowl to coat. Season to taste with salt and pepper.

3 Place a large flameproof skillet on the cooking grate. Add the almonds. Cook, with the lid closed as much as possible, stirring often, until toasted, about 3 minutes. Transfer to a plate. Add the butter, the remaining 2 tablespoons oil, the wine, and the lemon juice to the skillet and bring to a boil. Add the toasted almonds. Set aside.

4 Brush the cooking grate clean and generously oil the grate. Season the salmon fillets with ½ teaspoon salt and ½ teaspoon pepper. Place the fillets, skin-side down, on the grate. Add the asparagus to the grate, with the spears running perpendicular to the grid. Cook, with the lid closed as much as possible, occasionally rolling the asparagus on the grate to turn it, until the asparagus is crisp-tender, about 5 minutes. Transfer the asparagus to a platter and tent with aluminum foil to keep warm.

5 Continue grilling the salmon fillets until the skin has browned and you can lift the salmon with a metal spatula without the skin sticking, about 1 minute

more. Flip the fillets and cook just until the flesh is seared with grill marks, about 1 minute. Transfer the salmon to a platter.

6 Return the skillet to the grill and return the sauce to a simmer. Add the fillets, skin-side down, to the sauce. Cook until the salmon is barely opaque when the fillets are pierced in the thickest part with the tip of a sharp knife, about 3 minutes. Season the sauce to taste with salt and pepper. Using a slotted spatula, arrange the salmon on top of the asparagus on the platter, and spoon the sauce over both. Serve hot.

frutti di mare alla rao's

Makes 4 servings

Whenever I taste this wonderful dish, it evokes memories of an amazing meal I had overlooking the beach on the Amalfi coast in Naples. A delicious combination of five different kinds of seafood served in a basil-scented sauce, this recipe can also be savored as a pasta sauce.

1 (14.5-ounce) can whole Italian plum tomatoes, preferably San Marzano

¼ cup extra-virgin olive oil

6 garlic cloves, crushed under a knife and peeled

1 tablespoon finely chopped shallots

1 cup dry white wine

½ cup bottled clam juice

16 littleneck or cherrystone clams, scrubbed well

4 (5-ounce) cod fillets

4 jumbo (21/25 count) shrimp, peeled and deveined

4 calamari, cleaned, sacs cut crosswise into ½-inch rings, and tentacles coarsely chopped

8 ounces lump crabmeat, picked over for cartilage and shells

4 fresh basil leaves, hand-torn

1 tablespoon unsalted butter

Kosher salt

Freshly ground black pepper

¼ cup finely chopped fresh flat-leaf parsley

1 Prepare an outdoor grill for direct cooking over high heat (500°F).

2 Drain the tomatoes, and reserve ¼ cup of the juice. Crush the tomatoes with your hands. Set aside.

3 Place a large flameproof roasting pan on the cooking grate. Add the olive oil, garlic, and shallots and cook until softened, about 3 minutes. Stir in the tomatoes and the reserved juice, the wine, and clam juice. Add the clams, cod, shrimp, and calamari. Cover the pan with aluminum foil. Cook until the clams have opened and the other seafood is opaque, about 10 minutes. Using tongs and a slotted spoon, transfer the seafood to a platter and cover with foil to keep warm.

4 Add the crabmeat to the roasting pan and bring the cooking liquid to a boil. Cook until the liquid has reduced slightly, about 4 minutes. Remove from the heat. Add the basil and butter and stir until the butter melts. Season to taste with salt and pepper.

5 Divide the seafood evenly among four large bowls. Top each with equal amounts of sauce, sprinkle with parsley, and serve hot.

FRUTTI DI MARE DI AMALFI WITH SPAGHETTI:
There is another, equally delicious, way to serve this
wonderful seafood dish—with pasta. Cook 1 pound
spaghetti in lightly salted boiling water according to the
package directions until just short of al dente and drain
well. Add to the reduced tomato mixture in the pan and
cook, stirring often, until the pasta is al dente, about
3 minutes. Transfer the spaghetti and sauce to a large
bowl, top with the seafood, sprinkle with the parsley, and
serve hot.

pasta

NO MATTER WHAT TIME OF YEAR, PASTA IS A SATISFYING MEAL THAT everyone—and I mean everyone—loves. When the weather is hot, concentrate on tomatoes, basil, peas, and other seasonal produce and seafood to make pasta suppers that are appropriately light. I've timed these fast-and-easy pasta sauces to be ready by the time the water comes to a boil (if you have a side burner, cook the pasta outside) to get the food on the table in record time. Or cook the pasta just short of al dente a couple of hours ahead of time, drain, rinse, and toss with oil to be ready for a final saucing.

spaghetti
with crab and heirloom tomato

Makes 4 to 6 servings

This is a dish that was created on-the-fly in our Las Vegas restaurant when we had a bumper supply of juicy, sweet heirloom tomatoes on hand. If it's not summer, just use canned San Marzano tomatoes.

1 cup extra-virgin olive oil

3 garlic cloves, crushed under a knife and peeled

7 ripe heirloom tomatoes, cored and cut into quarters

Kosher salt

Freshly ground black pepper

½ pound lump crabmeat, picked through for cartilage and shells

⅔ cup dry white wine

1 pound spaghetti or linguine

2 tablespoons unsalted butter

⅓ cup packed basil leaves, torn by hand, plus more for garnish

½ teaspoon crushed hot red pepper flakes (optional)

1 lemon, halved, plus lemon wedges for garnish

1 Prepare an outdoor grill for direct cooking over high heat (500°F). Bring a large pot of salted water to a boil over high heat on the stovetop or on a gas grill.

2 Place a large flameproof skillet on the cooking grate. Add the oil and garlic. Cook, with the lid closed, until the oil shimmers, about 2 minutes. Carefully add the tomatoes to the skillet and season with 1 teaspoon salt and ½ teaspoon pepper. Cook, stirring occasionally, until the tomatoes are softened, about 5 minutes. Stir in half of the crabmeat. Simmer, stirring often, until the juices are slightly thickened, about 5 minutes more. Carefully stir in the wine. Cook until the liquid has thickened slightly again, about 6 minutes more. Remove the skillet from the heat.

3 Add the spaghetti to the boiling satled water and cook according to the package directions until al dente.

4 Return the skillet to the grill. Add the butter and basil leaves to the sauce and stir well. Add the red pepper flakes, if using, and the remaining crabmeat. Remove about ½ cup of the sauce from the skillet and reserve. Add the spaghetti to the skillet and cook, tossing with kitchen tongs, until it is al dente and well coated with the sauce, about 2 minutes more. Season to taste with salt and pepper. Transfer to a serving bowl and squeeze the juice of 1 lemon over it. Top with the reserved sauce. Garnish with more torn basil leaves. Serve hot with the lemon wedges.

spaghetti
con zucchini aglio e olio

Summer is the best time of the year for zucchini and yellow squash, so take advantage of it! The bright fresh vegetables are cooked only slightly to retain their bite, and pair well with a fruity extra-virgin olive oil. This is summer on a plate.

Makes 4 to 6 servings

1 Prepare an outdoor grill for direct cooking over medium-high heat (450°F). Bring a large pot of salted water to a boil over high heat on the stovetop or on the side burner of a gas grill.

2 Place a large flameproof skillet on the cooking grate. Add the oil, garlic, and red pepper flakes. Cook, with the lid closed as much as possible, until the oil shimmers, about 3 minutes. Add the zucchini and cook, stirring occasionally, until lightly browned around the edges, about 10 minutes. Season to taste with salt and black pepper. Remove the skillet from the heat.

3 Add the spaghetti to the boiling salted water and cook according to the package directions until al dente. Drain well.

4 Return the skillet with the squash mixture to the cooking grate. Add the drained spaghetti and cook, tossing the pasta with kitchen tongs, until the mixture is well combined, about 1 minute. Transfer to a serving bowl and serve hot.

1 cup extra-virgin olive oil

3 garlic cloves, crushed under a knife and peeled

Pinch of crushed hot red pepper flakes

5 zucchini (or 3 zucchini and 2 yellow squash), trimmed and cut into ⅛-inch rounds

Kosher salt

Freshly ground black pepper

1 pound spaghetti

linguine and clam zuppa

Makes 4 to 6 servings

This is another dish that works well for summer because it is so light and fresh. It is equally tasty without the pasta, served as an appetizer with crusty bread. It has both dried and fresh oregano, the first for its spiciness and the latter to supply freshness. This recipe also works nicely with mussels.

1 cup extra-virgin olive oil

2 garlic cloves, crushed under a knife and peeled

4 dozen littleneck clams, rinsed and scrubbed well

1½ teaspoons dried oregano

1 cup dry white wine

1 cup bottled clam juice

1 pound linguine or spaghetti

2 teaspoons coarsely chopped fresh oregano

2 fresh basil leaves, hand-torn

Kosher salt

Freshly ground black pepper

1 Prepare an outdoor grill for direct cooking over high heat (500°F). Bring a large pot of salted water to a boil over high heat on the stovetop or on the side burner of a gas grill.

2 Place a large flameproof roasting pan on the cooking grate. Add the oil and garlic. Cook, with the lid closed as much as possible, until the garlic is golden brown, about 3 minutes. Remove and discard the garlic with a slotted spoon. Add the clams and dried oregano. Pour in the wine and clam juice. Cover the pan with a lid or aluminum foil and cook, shaking the pan occasionally, until the clams open, about 10 minutes. Using tongs, transfer the clams to a platter and tent with aluminum foil to keep warm. Boil the liquid in the pan until it has reduced by one-third, about 5 minutes.

3 Meanwhile, cook the linguine in the boiling salted water according to the package directions until just al dente. Drain well. Add the linguine to the liquid in the roasting pan and cook, tossing with tongs, until the pasta absorbs a little sauce, about 1 minute. Stir in the fresh oregano and basil. Season with salt and pepper. Transfer the spaghetti and sauce to a deep serving bowl, top with the clams, and serve hot.

LINGUINE AND CLAM ZUPPA WITH TOMATOES:
Add 5 fresh ripe plum tomatoes, seeded and diced (or 5 drained canned San Marzano tomatoes, hand-crushed), to the pan with the wine and clam juice.

penne with peas and ham

Makes
4 to 6
servings

While it is fine to use frozen peas here, this is the pasta to make when you run across fresh peas at a farmers' market. Allow about 2 pounds of peas in the shell for 2 cups of shelled peas. Just shuck the peas and cook them until tender in boiling salted water, about 5 minutes.

¼ cup extra-virgin olive oil

3 whole garlic cloves, crushed under a knife and peeled

⅓ cup finely chopped onion

1 cup ½-inch-dice smoked ham

2 cups cooked fresh or thawed frozen peas

1 cup canned reduced-sodium chicken broth

Kosher salt

Freshly ground pepper

1 pound penne

¼ cup freshly grated Parmigiano-Reggiano cheese, plus more for serving

1 Prepare an outdoor grill for direct cooking over high heat (550°F). Bring a large pot of salted water to a boil over high heat on the stovetop or on the side burner of a gas grill.

2 Place a large flameproof skillet on the cooking grate. Add the oil and garlic and cook, with the lid closed as much as possible, until the garlic shimmers, about 2 minutes. Add the onion and cook until softened, about 3 minutes. Stir in the ham and cook, stirring often, until the onion is translucent, 3 to 5 minutes. Stir in the peas and cook until they are heated through, about 3 minutes. Add the broth and bring to a boil. Cook until the liquid has reduced by half, about 5 minutes. Season to taste with salt and pepper. Remove the skillet from the heat.

3 Add the penne to the boiling salted water and cook according to the package directions until al dente. Drain well. Return it to the cooking pot. Add the pea mixture along with the grated cheese and toss well. Transfer to a serving bowl and serve hot with additional cheese passed on the side.

linguine with tuna sauce

You may have heard the advice to never put cheese on seafood. This may be because the people of the seaside regions in Italy lived on the food from the sea rather than livestock, as there wasn't a lot of grazing land. Whatever the reason, here is a terrific pasta with tuna sauce that is finished off with bread crumbs.

Makes 6 servings

1 Prepare an outdoor grill for direct cooking over high heat (550°F). Bring a large pot of salted water to a boil over high heat on the stovetop or on the side burner of a gas grill.

2 Place a large flameproof skillet on the cooking grate and add the oil and garlic. Cook, with the lid closed as much as possible, until the garlic softens, about 2 minutes. Stir in the olives and tuna. Cook, stirring occasionally, until the tuna is heated through, about 3 minutes. Stir in the capers. Add the wine and bring to a boil. Reduce the heat on a gas grill to medium-low (350°F). On a charcoal grill, move the skillet to the edge of the grate not directly over the coals. Simmer until the sauce has reduced by half, about 3 minutes. Squeeze in the lemon juice, add the parsley, and stir. Add the butter and stir until it is melted.

3 Meanwhile, add the linguine to the boiling salted water and cook according to the package directions until just short of al dente. Drain and rinse under cold running water. Drain well.

4 Add the linguine to the skillet and cook, occasionally tossing with tongs, until the linguine is cooked to al dente and coated with the sauce, about 2 minutes. Season to taste with salt and pepper. Sprinkle with the bread crumbs. Transfer to a serving bowl, and serve hot.

¼ cup exta-virgin olive oil

1 teaspoon minced garlic

1 cup pitted black Mediterranean olives, such as Kalamata

2 (5- to 6-ounce) cans tuna in oil, preferably Italian tuna in olive oil, drained

1 tablespoon drained capers

½ cup dry white wine

2 tablespoons freshly squeezed lemon juice

1 tablespoon finely chopped fresh flat-leaf parsley

1 tablespoon unsalted butter

1 pound linguine

Kosher salt

Freshly ground black pepper

1½ tablespoons plain dried bread crumbs

linguine with shrimp and arugula

Makes
4 to 6
servings

Arugula is well known as a salad ingredient, but its peppery flavor can really spice up pasta, too. Be sure to rinse it very well, as it is always sandy. For a quick shrimp stock, reserve the shells from peeling the shrimp, and simmer the shells in 1 cup canned reduced-sodium chicken broth for 10 minutes, then strain.

¼ cup extra-virgin olive oil, plus more for serving

2 garlic cloves, thinly sliced

½ pound jumbo (21/25 count) shrimp, peeled and deveined

1 cup dry white wine

1 pint cherry tomatoes, halved

1 cup shrimp stock (see above), bottled clam juice, or canned reduced-sodium chicken broth

1 pound linguine

2 cups packed arugula leaves, torn into bite-size pieces

1 Prepare an outdoor grill for direct cooking over high heat (500°F). Bring a large pot of salted water to a boil over high heat on the stovetop or on the side burner of a gas grill.

2 Place a large flameproof skillet on the cooking grate. Add the oil and garlic. Cook, with the lid closed as much as possible, until the garlic shimmers, about 2 minutes. Add the shrimp and cook just until they turn opaque, about 4 minutes. Using a slotted spoon, transfer the shrimp to a plate and set aside. Add the wine to the skillet, bring to a boil, and cook for 1 minute. Add the cherry tomatoes and shrimp stock and cook until the tomatoes are heated through, about 3 minutes. Remove the skillet from the heat.

3 Meanwhile, add the linguine to the boiling salted water and cook according to the package directions until barely al dente. Drain well.

4 Return the skillet to the grill. Add the linguine, shrimp, and arugula to the skillet. Cook, tossing with kitchen tongs, until the pasta is well coated with the sauce, about 1 minute. Season to taste with salt and pepper. Transfer to a serving bowl, drizzle with additional olive oil, and serve hot.

pizza
and friends

WHO DOESN'T LIKE PIZZA? WE STARTED SERVING PIZZAS AT RAO'S at Caesars Palace for lunch and they are a huge hit. We know that not everyone has a wood-fired pizza oven in their backyard, but a pizza on the grill is a thing of wonder, and the high heat gives the dough that pizzeria flavor. I find that grilling the dough on a perforated pizza pan is an enormous help. And don't forget pizza's cousins, the half-round calzone and the rolled-up stromboli.

pizza dough

Makes enough dough for two 12-inch pizzas

While you can use store-bought pizza dough, there is such satisfaction in making your own. Here is a dough that grills into a crisp and chewy crust. It uses supermarket unbleached all-purpose flour, but I am a fan of Italian "00" flour for pizza dough. It is available at many Italian specialty food stores or online.

1½ cups lukewarm (105° to 115°F) water, or more as needed

1 (¼-ounce) envelope active dry yeast

1 teaspoon sugar

4 cups unbleached all-purpose flour (see Headnote), as needed

1 teaspoon kosher salt

1 tablespoon extra-virgin olive oil, plus more for the bowl, if making dough by hand

1 **To make the dough by hand:** Pour the lukewarm water into a medium bowl. Sprinkle in the yeast and sugar and let stand until the yeast softens and the mixture looks active (it may or may not bubble), about 5 minutes. Stir to dissolve the yeast. Put the flour in a large bowl. Gradually add the yeast mixture to the flour, mixing with your hands to combine. Add the oil and mix until the dough is soft and sticky. If the dough is dry, add a little more water, or add flour if it is too wet. Turn the dough out onto a lightly floured work surface and knead until smooth and elastic, about 10 minutes, adding more flour as needed. If using this method, skip to step 3.

2 **To make the dough with a heavy-duty stand mixer:** Combine the lukewarm water, yeast, and sugar in the mixer bowl. Let stand until the yeast softens and the mixture looks active (it may or may not bubble), 5 to 10 minutes. Stir to dissolve the yeast. Affix the bowl to the mixer fitted with the paddle attachment. With the machine on low speed, gradually add enough of the flour to make a rough dough. Switch the paddle attachment for the dough hook. Knead on medium-low speed, adding more flour as needed, until the dough is smooth and elastic, about 10 minutes.

3 Oil a large bowl. Shape the dough into a ball, place it in the bowl, and turn the dough to coat with oil. Cover the bowl with plastic wrap or a dampened kitchen towel. Let stand in a warm place until it has almost

doubled in volume, approximately 90 minutes. Deflate the dough in the bowl with your fist, cover again, and let rise for 1 hour more.

4 Turn out the dough onto a work surface. Cut in half, and shape each half into a ball. Place each half in a 1-gallon ziplock bag and refrigerate until ready to use, up to 8 hours. (Or wrap each ball of dough in plastic wrap, slip into a plastic bag, and freeze for up to 1 month; thaw overnight in the refrigerator before using.) If the dough is chilled, let it stand at room temperature for 30 minutes before shaping.

pizza sauce

This reliable recipe makes enough sauce for two pizzas or more than enough as a dip for calzones or stromboli. San Marzano tomatoes, which are grown in volcanic soil near Naples, do make a difference, as they have a meaty texture that other varieties lack. The very best brands are labeled *Pomodoro San Marzano dell'Agro Sarnese-Nocerino*, which means that they come from the Valle de Sarno region.

2 tablespoons extra-virgin olive oil

1 garlic clove, minced

1 (28-ounce) can San Marzano tomatoes, with their juices, well crushed by hand

1 teaspoon kosher salt

1 teaspoon dried oregano

½ teaspoon freshly ground black pepper

3 or 4 whole fresh basil leaves

1 Heat the oil in a large skillet over medium heat. Add the garlic and cook until softened, without browning, about 1 minute. Add the tomatoes with their juices and sprinkle with the salt. Bring to a boil, stirring often. Reduce the heat to medium-low.

2 Add the oregano, pepper, and basil. Simmer, stirring occasionally, until the tomato juices are thick, 15 to 20 minutes. Transfer to a bowl and let cool completely.

basic pizza on the grill

Here are the instructions for a basic pizza, to which you can add any of the toppings as directed in the recipes that follow. Be sure that the grill temperature is not too high, or the dough will burn before it has a chance to cook through. A perforated metal pizza pan, lightly oiled to prevent sticking, will take much of the stress out of your grilled-pizza making. If you wish, you can prepare the pizza rounds one after the other, but I like to make and bake one pizza at a time, because once the pizza is pregrilled, the finishing only takes a few minutes.

Makes two 12-inch pizza crusts

1 Prepare an outdoor grill for direct cooking over medium-high heat (450°F). Lightly oil a 14-inch perforated metal pizza pan.

2 On a lightly floured work surface, press and shape 1 ball of the pizza dough into a thick round. With a rolling pin, roll out the dough into a 12-inch round and stretch and pat the dough, as needed, to get it into shape. Slide the dough onto the pizza pan. Drizzle olive oil over the dough.

3 Generously oil the cooking grate. Place the pan on the grate. Grill, with the lid closed as much as possible, until the dough looks set, 2 to 3 minutes. Slide the dough off the pan onto the grate. Cook until the dough is cooked through, 2 to 3 minutes more. Using the pizza pan or a rimless cookie sheet, remove the pizza crust from the grill and set aside. Repeat the procedure with the second ball of dough. The pizza is now ready for your favorite toppings. Use immediately or set aside, uncovered, at room temperature, for up to 1 hour.

Extra-virgin olive oil for the pan and for drizzling

Unbleached all-purpose flour for shaping the dough

Pizza Dough (page 104)

pizza alla rao's

Makes two
12-inch
pizzas

This pizza touches all the bases—tomatoes, garlic, cheese, and fresh basil—and then slides in for a home run. What else do you need? Sausage and pepperoni lovers, your turn will come. . . .

Olive oil for the pan

Basic Pizza on the Grill (2 pizza crusts, page 107)

1 cup Pizza Sauce (page 106)

4 tablespoons freshly grated Parmigiano-Reggiano cheese

1 pound fresh mozzarella cheese, cut into thin rounds, or shredded processed mozzarella

10 fresh basil leaves

1 Prepare an outdoor grill for direct cooking over medium heat (350°F). Lightly oil a 14-inch perforated pizza pan.

2 Place the first pizza dough on the pan and grill, with the lid closed as much as possible, until the underside is heated, about 1 minute. Flip the dough on the pan and heat the opposite side, about 1 minute longer. Flip again and spread ½ cup of pizza sauce on dough. Sprinkle with 2 tablespoons of the grated Parmigiano-Reggiano. Put half of the mozzarella and half of the basil leaves on top. Close the grill and continue cooking until the cheese has melted, about 2 minutes. Using the pizza pan or a rimless cookie sheet, remove the pizza from the grill and transfer to a serving platter or chopping board. Let stand for a few minutes, then slice and serve. Repeat the procedure with the remaining ingredients to make the second pizza.

sausage pizza

For those of you who like meat on your pizza, this one's for you. I'm not going to tell you if hot sausage, sweet sausage, or pepperoni is better than the other—you know what you like. One warning: Don't overload the pizza with meat, or it will drop when you pick it up.

Makes two 12-inch pizzas

1 Prepare an outdoor grill for direct cooking over medium-high heat (450°F).

2 Brush the cooking grate clean. Put the sausages on the cooking grate. Grill the sausages, with the lid closed as much as possible, turning occasionally, until firm and cooked through, about 10 minutes. Transfer to a chopping board and let cool until easy to handle. Cut into ¼-inch-thick rounds. Set aside.

3 Reduce the grill temperature to medium heat (350°F). Lightly oil a 14-inch perforated pizza pan.

4 Place the first pizza dough on the pan and grill, with the lid closed as much as possible, until the underside is heated, about 2 to 3 minutes. Flip the dough on the pan and heat the opposite side, about 1 to 2 minutes longer. Flip again and spread ½ cup of pizza sauce on dough. Sprinkle with 2 tablespoons of grated Parmigiano-Reggiano. Arrange half of the mozzarella and half of the sausage rounds on top. Close the grill and continue cooking until the cheese has melted, about 2 minutes. Using the pizza pan or a rimless cookie sheet, remove the pizza from the grill and transfer to a serving platter or chopping board. Let stand for a few minutes, then slice and serve. Repeat the procedure with the remaining ingredients to make the second pizza.

3 sweet or hot Italian sausage links (about 9 ounces), pricked with a fork

Olive oil for the pan

Basic Pizza on the Grill (2 pizza crusts, page 107)

1 cup Pizza Sauce (page 106)

4 tablespoons freshly grated Parmigiano-Reggiano cheese

1 pound fresh mozzarella cheese, cut into thin rounds, or use shredded processed mozzarella

PEPPERONI PIZZA Substitute 6 ounces sliced pepperoni for the sausage. Do not cook the pepperoni, just add half to each pizza after sprinkling with the grated cheese.

four-cheese pizza

Makes two 12-inch pizzas

Mozzarella isn't the only cheese that makes great pizza. It shares space in this pie with Fontina and Gruyère, and all three are topped with a sprinkle of sharp Gorgonzola. A drizzle of truffle oil finishes it all off for a touch of elegance.

Olive oil for the pan

Basic Pizza on the Grill (2 pizza crusts, page 107)

8 ounces fresh mozzarella, cut into thin rounds, or use shredded processed mozzarella

¾ cup (3 ounces) shredded Fontina cheese, preferably Fontina valle d'Aosta

¾ cup (3 ounces) shredded Gruyère cheese

½ cup (2 ounces) crumbled Gorgonzola cheese

Truffle oil for serving

Freshly ground black pepper for serving

1 Prepare an outdoor grill for direct cooking over medium heat (350°F). Lightly oil a 14-inch perforated pizza pan.

2 Place the first pizza dough on the pan and grill, with the lid closed as much as possible, until the underside is heated, about 1 minute. Flip the dough on the pan and heat the opposite side, about 1 minute longer. Flip again. Visually separate the pizza dough into thirds. Using half of the mozzarella, Fontina, and Gruyère, place each cheese in its own third on the pizza dough. Sprinkle half of the Gorgonzola on top. Close the grill and continue cooking until the cheese has melted, about 2 minutes. Using the pizza pan or a rimless cookie sheet, remove the pizza from the grill and transfer to a serving platter or chopping board. Let stand for a few minutes. Drizzle truffle oil over the pizza and top with a few grinds of pepper. Slice and serve. Repeat the procedure with the remaining ingredients to make the second pizza.

four seasons pizza

Makes two 12-inch pizzas This pizza, with four separate "compartments" of toppings, is very popular in European pizzerias, and deserves more exposure here. It has something for everyone.

Olive oil for the pan

Basic Pizza on the Grill (2 pizza crusts, page 107)

1 cup Pizza Sauce (page 106)

4 tablespoons freshly grated Parmigiano-Reggiano cheese

8 ounces fresh mozzarella cheese, cut into thin rounds, or use shredded processed mozzarella

⅔ cup thawed and coarsely chopped frozen artichoke hearts, patted dry with paper towels

⅔ cup pitted and coarsely chopped black olives

1 cup very thinly sliced white button mushrooms

2 ounces paper-thin slices prosciutto

1 Prepare an outdoor grill for direct cooking over medium heat (350°F). Lightly oil a 14-inch perforated pizza pan.

2 Place the first pizza dough on the pan and grill, with the lid closed as much as possible, until the underside is heated, about 1 minute. Flip the dough on the pan and heat the opposite side, about 1 to 2 minutes longer. Flip again and spread ½ cup of pizza sauce on dough. Sprinkle with 2 tablespoons of the Parmigiano-Reggiano, followed by half of the mozzarella. Visually separate the pizza dough into quarters. Using half of the artichoke hearts, olives, mushrooms, and prosciutto, and folding the prosciutto to fit into its space, arrange each ingredient in its own quadrant on the pizza dough. Close the grill and continue cooking until the mozzarella has melted, 2 to 3 minutes. Using the pizza pan or a rimless cookie sheet, remove the pizza from the grill and transfer to a serving platter or chopping board. Let stand for a few minutes. Slice and serve. Repeat the procedure with the remaining ingredients to make the second pizza.

sausage and ricotta pizza

Ricotta adds a rich creaminess to pizza. Fresh ricotta can be found at many Italian delicatessens, so when you find it, use it to make this special "white" pie.

Makes two 12-inch pizzas

1 Prepare an outdoor grill for direct cooking over medium-high heat (450°F).

2 Brush the cooking grate clean and oil the grate. Put the sausages on the grate. Grill the sausages, with the lid closed as much as possible, turning occasionally, until firm and cooked through, about 10 minutes. Transfer to a chopping board and let cool until easy to handle. Cut into ¼-inch-thick rounds. Set aside.

3 Reduce the grill temperature to medium heat (350°F). Lightly oil a 14-inch perforated pizza pan.

4 Place the first pizza dough on the pan and grill, with the lid closed as much as possible, until the underside is heated, about 1 minute. Flip the dough on the pan and heat the opposite side, about 1 minute longer. Flip again and arrange half of the mozzarella over the pizza dough. Using half of the ricotta, spoon 6 dollops of the ricotta onto the pizza. Scatter half of the sausage rounds on top. Close the grill and continue cooking until the cheese has melted, about 2 minutes. Using the pizza pan or rimless baking sheet, remove the pizza from the grill and transfer to a serving platter or chopping board. Let stand for a few minutes. Sprinkle 2 teaspoons of rosemary over the pizza, slice, and serve. Repeat the procedure with the remaining ingredients to make the second pizza.

3 sweet or hot Italian sausage links, each pierced with a fork

Olive oil for the pan

Basic Pizza on the Grill (2 pizza crusts, page 107)

8 ounces fresh mozzarella cheese, cut into thin rounds, or use shredded processed mozzarella

1⅓ cups whole-milk ricotta cheese

4 teaspoons finely chopped fresh rosemary for sprinkling

broccoli rabe white pizza

Makes two 12-inch pizzas

Broccoli rabe (also called rapini) looks like broccoli, but it has its own distinct bitter flavor that goes very well with garlic. A brief blanching tames the broccoli rabe's rough edges.

1 pound broccoli rabe

2 tablespoons extra-virgin olive oil, plus more for the pan

3 garlic cloves, thinly sliced

Basic Pizza on the Grill (2 pizza crusts, page 107)

8 ounces fresh mozzarella cheese, cut into thin rounds, or use shredded processed mozzarella

1⅔ cups whole-milk ricotta cheese

1 Bring a large pot of salted water to a boil. Rinse the broccoli rabe well to remove grit—it can be sandy. Shake off the excess water, but do not dry. Add to the boiling water and cook until it turns bright green, about 5 minutes. Drain and rinse under cold running water. Drain well. Pat with paper towels to remove excess water, then coarsely chop it.

2 Heat the olive oil and garlic in a large skillet over medium heat until the garlic turns golden. Add the broccoli rabe and cover. Reduce the heat to medium-low and cook, stirring occasionally, until the broccoli rabe is tender, about 10 minutes. Uncover during the last few minutes to evaporate any excess water. Drain in a colander. Let cool.

3 Prepare an outdoor grill for direct cooking over medium-high heat (450°F). Lightly oil a 14-inch perforated pizza pan.

4 Place the first pizza dough on the pan and grill, with the lid closed as much as possible, until heated, about 1 minute. Flip the dough on the pan and heat the opposite side, about 1 minute longer. Flip again and arrange half of the mozzarella over the dough. Scatter half of the broccoli rabe with any clinging garlic slices on top, followed by half of the ricotta in 6 dollops. Close the grill and continue cooking until the cheese has melted, about 2 to 4 minutes. Using the pizza pan, remove the pizza from the grill and transfer to a platter or chopping board. Let stand for a few minutes. Slice and serve.

ham calzone

Calzone means "trouser leg" in Italian because the edge of the folded crust looks like a pants cuff. This big pizza turnover is fun to make and equally fun to eat by dipping the corner of your piece into tomato sauce.

Makes 2 calzones, 2 or 3 servings each

1 Prepare an outdoor grill for direct cooking over medium-high heat (450°F). Lightly oil a 14-inch perforated metal pizza pan.

2 On a lightly floured work surface, press and shape 1 ball of the pizza dough into a thick round. With a rolling pin, roll out the dough into a 12-inch round and stretch and pat the dough, as needed, to get it into shape. Slide the dough onto the pizza pan.

3 Drop 1 cup of ricotta in dollops over the bottom half of the dough round, leaving a ½-inch border around the bottom edge of the dough. Sprinkle with ½ cup of the ham. Lightly brush the bottom edge of the dough with water. Fold the dough over, press together the open edges, and trim off the thin dough at the edges. Pierce a ½-inch-wide slit in the top of the dough with the tip of a knife to let the steam escape during baking.

4 Generously oil the cooking grate. Place the pan on the grate. Grill, with the lid closed as much as possible, until the dough is set, about 5 minutes. Cook until the calzone is golden brown, 2 to 3 minutes. Remove the calzone from the grill and slide onto a serving platter or chopping board. Let stand for a few minutes. Brush with half of the melted butter. Cut into 3 or 4 pieces and serve with bowls of the pizza sauce for dipping.

5 Repeat the procedure with the remaining ingredients to make the second calzone.

Olive oil for the pan

Pizza Dough (page 104)

2 cups whole-milk ricotta cheese

1 cup ½-inch-dice smoked ham

2 tablespoons unsalted butter, melted, for brushing

Pizza Sauce (page 106), heated, for dipping

meatball calzone

Makes 2
calzones,
2 or 3
servings each

The next time you have leftover meatballs and spaghetti sauce, use them as a calzone filling. Or pick up a couple of meatballs from the deli and a jar of our Rao's Homemade Marinara Sauce and go from there. If you use fresh mozzarella, freeze the ball for about an hour to firm it up before shredding.

Olive oil for the pan

Pizza Dough (page 104)

2 cups (8 ounces) shredded fresh or processed mozzarella cheese

2 large (6 ounces each) meatballs, cut in halves and sliced ¼-inch thick

2½ cups Rao's Homemade Marinara Sauce, your favorite pasta sauce, or Pizza Sauce (page 106)

2 tablespoons unsalted butter, melted, for brushing

1 Prepare an outdoor grill for direct cooking over medium-high heat (450°F). Lightly oil a 14-inch perforated metal pizza pan.

2 On a lightly floured work surface, press and shape 1 ball of the pizza dough into a thick round. With a rolling pin, roll out the dough into a 12-inch round and stretch and pat the dough, as needed, to get it into shape. Slide the dough onto the pizza pan.

3 Scatter half of the mozzarella over the bottom half of the dough round, leaving a ½-inch border around the bottom edge of the dough. Top with half of the sliced meatballs and dollop with ¼ cup of the marinara sauce. Lightly brush the bottom edge of the dough with water. Fold the dough over, press together the open edges, and trim off the thin dough at the edges. Pierce a ½-inch-wide slit in the top of the dough with the tip of a knife to let the steam escape during baking.

4 Generously oil the cooking grate. Place the pan on the grate. Grill, with the lid closed as much as possible, until the dough is set, about 5 minutes. Slide the dough off the pan onto the grate. Cook until the calzone is golden brown, 2 to 3 minutes. Remove the calzone from the grill and slide onto a serving platter or chopping board. Let stand for a few minutes.

(recipe continues)

5 While the calzone is resting, set aside ¼ cup of the sauce for the second pizza. Reheat the remaining 2 cups of the sauce in a saucepan over medium heat (or on the grill side burner), and transfer to small bowls for dipping. Brush the calzone with half of the melted butter. Cut into 3 or 4 pieces and serve with the sauce.

6 Repeat the procedure with the remaining ingredients to make the second calzone.

sausage and pepper stromboli

Makes 2 stromboli, 4 servings each

This rolled-up pizza is a great dish for a party because it is easier to eat than sliced pizza. You'll need to make a batch of Peppers and Onions (page 126), or use the leftover sausage and vegetables from Grilled Sausages with Peppers and Onions on page 44.

Olive oil for the pan

Pizza Dough (page 104)

2 cups (8 ounces) shredded processed mozzarella

4 cooked hot or sweet sausages (see step 2, page 113), sliced into ½-inch-thick rounds

1 cup Peppers and Onions (page 126), cooled

2 tablespoons unsalted butter, melted, for brushing

1 Prepare an outdoor grill for direct cooking over medium-high heat (450°F). Lightly oil a 14-inch perforated metal pizza pan.

2 On a lightly floured work surface, press and shape 1 ball of pizza dough into a thick rectangle. With a rolling pin, roll out the dough into a 9 x 5-inch rectangle. Slide the dough onto the pizza pan.

3 Scatter 1 cup of the cheese over the dough, leaving a ½-inch border around the top and bottom edges of the dough. Top with half of the sausage rounds and half of the peppers and onions. Lightly brush the bottom edge of the dough with water. Starting at the bottom, roll up the dough, and pinch the seam closed. Turn the stromboli so the seam is on the bottom. Leave the ends open and unsealed. Pierce a ½-inch-wide slit in the top of the dough with the tip of a knife to let the steam escape during baking.

4 Generously oil the cooking grate. Place the pan on the grate. Grill, with the lid closed as much as possible, until the dough is set, about 5 minutes. Slide the dough off the pan onto the grate. Cook until the underside is golden brown, about 4 minutes. Carefully flip the stromboli over and cook until the opposite side is browned, about 4 minutes longer. Transfer the stromboli to a cutting board. Let stand a few minutes. Brush with half of the melted butter, cut crosswise into thick slices, and serve.

garlic bread

Regardless of whether your meal is served indoors or out, garlic bread goes so well with so many dishes. Benefiting from a final toasting on the grill, this version delivers an extra-crisp crust with buttery and garlicky insides.

Makes 6 servings

1 Prepare an outdoor grill for direct cooking over medium heat (400°F).

2 Split the bread horizontally with a serrated knife. Drizzle the olive oil over the cut sides of the bread halves. Spread each half evenly with the butter, then the garlic. Put the halves back together and wrap in aluminum foil.

3 Place the wrapped bread on the cooking grate. Grill, with the lid closed as much as possible, turning halfway through the grilling, until the bread is heated, about 8 minutes. Unwrap the bread, being careful not to let any of the melted butter drip onto the heat source, which can cause flare-ups. Place the bread halves, crust-side down, on the cooking grate.

4 Grill until the crust is very crisp and browning in spots, about 3 minutes. Transfer to a chopping board. Cut crosswise into 1-inch-thick slices, transfer to a serving bowl, and serve hot.

1 oblong loaf crusty Italian bread

¼ cup extra-virgin olive oil

6 tablespoons (¾ stick) salted butter, at room temperature

6 tablespoons minced garlic

vegetables

NEVER TAKE VEGETABLES FOR GRANTED OR TREAT THEM AS AN afterthought—they are an important part of the meal for many reasons. Outside of their health benefits, they add color and variety to the table. These are uncomplicated recipes to show off the flavors of summer produce at its best. Head off to your local farmers' market and let the bounty inspire you.

grilled artichokes
with spicy lemon dip

Makes 4 servings

Grilling really brings out the flavor of artichokes, but allow time for par-cooking before they are put on the grill. I've given a recipe for a dipping sauce, but use your favorite sauce (mayonnaise or melted butter are both popular) for dipping the leaves.

DIPPING SAUCE

¾ cup extra-virgin olive oil

Juice of 1 lemon

1 teaspoon minced garlic

¼ teaspoon kosher salt

¼ teaspoon crushed hot red pepper flakes

4 artichokes

2 lemons, halved

¼ cup extra-virgin olive oil

Kosher salt

Freshly ground black pepper

1 Bring a large pot of salted water to a boil over high heat.

2 **To make the dipping sauce:** Whisk the ingredients together in a small bowl. Let stand at room temperature while cooking the artichokes.

3 For each artichoke, if the stem is attached, cut it off at the base. Rub the cut area with a lemon half. Using kitchen scissors, snip off the thorny tips of the leaves. Snap off the small, tough outer leaves. Rub the artichoke all over with the lemon half.

4 Place squeezed lemon halves into the boiling water. Add the artichokes and boil until they turn olive green, about 7 minutes. Drain and rinse under cold running water. Transfer to a bowl of ice water and let cool completely. Drain again and pat dry with paper towels. Using a large knife, cut each artichoke in half lengthwise. Remove the choke from each half by scraping it out with the edge of a soupspoon. Pat dry to remove water from the inner leaves. Transfer to a large bowl. Drizzle with the oil, sprinkle with ½ teaspoon salt and ½ teaspoon pepper, and toss to coat.

5 Prepare an outdoor grill for direct cooking over medium-high heat (450°F).

6 Brush the cooking grate clean. Place the artichokes, cut-side down, on the grate. Grill, with the lid closed as much as possible, until seared with grill marks, about 3 minutes. Rotate 90 degrees, and cook to sear with crosshatch marks, about 3 minutes more. Flip the artichokes and continue grilling until the leaves can be easily pulled off an artichoke half, about 6 minutes more. Season to taste with salt and pepper. Transfer to a platter and serve with your favorite sauce for dipping the leaves. Be sure to put out an empty bowl for collecting the scraped leaves.

grill-roasted beets with arugula

Makes 4 to 6 servings

Beets had a bad reputation until home cooks learned to roast, instead of boil, them. This is a side dish on its way to being a salad. You could crumble some *caprini* (goat cheese) on top if you wish. If you're a neatnik, you may want to wear rubber or latex gloves when peeling the cooked beets—to avoid staining your fingers red.

6 medium beets, trimmed

4 cups packed arugula leaves

2 tablespoons balsamic vinegar

¼ cup extra-virgin olive oil

Kosher salt

Freshly ground black pepper

1 Prepare an outdoor grill for direct cooking over medium-high heat (450°F).

2 Wrap each beet in aluminum foil. Put the beets on the cooking grate. Grill, with the lid closed as much as possible, turning the beets occasionally, until they are tender and can be pierced through the foil with a meat fork, about 45 minutes. Remove from the grill and let cool. Slip the peels off the beets and discard. Cut the beets into ½-inch-thick rounds.

3 Toss the arugula, 1 tablespoon of the vinegar, and 2 tablespoons of the oil in a large bowl. Season with salt and pepper and toss again. Spread on a serving platter. Arrange the beets on top and drizzle with the remaining 1 tablespoon vinegar and 2 tablespoons oil. Season to taste with salt and pepper and serve.

grilled corn on the cob

For many of us, it isn't a grill-out without corn on the cob. Grilled corn is even better than the familiar boiled corn, as the direct heat of the grill lightly caramelizes the kernels to bring out their sweetness.

Makes 6 servings

1 Peel back the husks from the corn, but keep the leaves attached to the end. Discard the corn silk tassels. Transfer the ears of corn to a large pot of salted water. Soak for at least 30 minutes and up to 2 hours.

2 Drain the corn and pat dry with kitchen towels. Spread the ears of corn with equal amounts of the softened butter, and season to taste with salt and pepper. Return the husks to their original positions.

3 Prepare an outdoor grill for direct cooking over medium-high heat (450°F).

4 Brush the cooking grate clean. Place the ears of corn on the grate. Grill, with the lid closed as much as possible, turning occasionally, until the husks are evenly browned and the ears inside the husks are hot and lightly browned in spots (open a husk to see if the corn is steaming), about 15 minutes. Transfer to a platter.

5 Let stand for 10 to 15 minutes to cool slightly. Remove and discard the husks; if the corn is too hot, protect your hands with kitchen towels. Serve the corn hot.

6 ears unhusked corn

8 tablespoons (1 stick) salted butter, at room temperature

Kosher salt

Freshly ground black pepper

peppers and onions

Makes
4 to 6
servings

This condiment will go with just about anything, starting from its classic pairing with grilled sausages to a topping for burgers and sandwiches. Sometimes, before we have settled on the meat for the main course, we will start the meal by cooking peppers and onions and go from there.

3 red and yellow bell peppers, in any combination, cored, seeded, and cut into ½-inch-wide strips

3 medium white onions, cut into ¼-inch-thick half-moons

⅓ cup extra-virgin olive oil

3 garlic cloves, crushed and peeled

1 teaspoon kosher salt

½ teaspoon freshly ground black pepper

1 Prepare an outdoor grill for direct cooking over medium-high heat (450°F).

2 Toss the peppers, onions, oil, and garlic in a large flameproof roasting pan. Season with the salt and pepper.

3 Put the pan on the cooking grate. Cook, stirring occasionally, until the onions are translucent and the peppers are crisp-tender, 20 to 25 minutes. Transfer to a serving bowl and serve warm or let cool to room temperature.

roasted potatoes on the grill

Potatoes go with any kind of grilled meat, so it's a good thing to know how to make them on the grill. With a little space management, the potatoes fit on one side of the grill and the meat on the other side. These are simple and delicious.

Makes
4 to 6
servings

1 Prepare an outdoor grill for direct cooking over high heat (500°F).

2 Combine the oil and garlic in a large flameproof roasting pan. Put the pan on the cooking grate. Grill, with the lid closed as much as possible, until the garlic begins to shimmer, about 2 minutes. Add the potatoes and stir to coat with the oil.

3 Grill, with the lid closed as much as possible, occasionally stirring and turning the potatoes with a metal spatula, until they are golden brown and tender, 20 to 25 minutes. Season to taste with salt and pepper. Using a slotted spoon, transfer the potatoes to a serving bowl and serve hot.

½ cup extra-virgin olive oil

3 garlic cloves, crushed and peeled

6 unpeeled waxy potatoes, each quartered lengthwise

Kosher salt

Freshly ground black pepper

two-hour rosemary potatoes

Makes 4
servings

These potatoes were born purely by accident. Once when grilling, I put potatoes on the top rack of the grill, cooked the meat, and forgot all about the potatoes. When I finally remembered them, they had been grilling for about two hours. I expected them to be burned, but they were crunchy on the outside and tender inside. I added a little olive oil and rosemary with a sprinkle of salt, and they were perfect.

4 large baking potatoes, such as Russet or Burbank, scrubbed but unpeeled

¼ cup extra-virgin olive oil

1 tablespoon chopped fresh rosemary

Kosher salt

Freshly ground black pepper.

1 Prepare an outdoor grill for direct cooking over medium-high heat (450°F). Wrap each potato in aluminum foil.

2 Place the potatoes in the upper warming basket while the grill preheats. Close the grill lid and cook until the potatoes feel tender when squeezed through the foil, about 1¼ hours, more or less, depending on the size of the potatoes.

3 Unwrap the potatoes and return them to the basket. Close the grill and cook the potatoes until the skin is dry and crispy, 10 minutes more.

4 Transfer the potatoes to a chopping board and coarsely chop them. Transfer to a serving bowl. While the potatoes are hot, drizzle with the oil and sprinkle with the rosemary. Season to taste with salt and pepper and serve.

frank sr.'s grilled potatoes

At the Rao family's backyard cookouts, these are the first side dish to disappear from the table. Thanks, Frank Sr., for this simple recipe. Make a lot so you aren't left empty-handed when people come back for seconds.

Makes 4 to 6 servings

1 Prepare an outdoor grill for direct cooking over medium-high heat (450°F).

2 In a large bowl, toss the potato wedges with the oil, oregano, garlic powder, salt, and pepper, making sure that the potatoes are evenly coated. Spread the potatoes in a single layer in a large flameproof roasting pan. Drizzle any remaining oil from the bowl over the potatoes.

3 Put the pan on the cooking grate. Grill, with the lid closed as much as possible, occasionally stirring and turning the potatoes with a metal spatula, until the potatoes are golden brown and tender, about 45 minutes. Using a slotted spoon, transfer the potatoes to a serving bowl and serve hot.

4 baking potatoes, such as Russet or Burbank, scrubbed but unpeeled, cut lengthwise into eighths

½ cup extra-virgin olive oil

2 teaspoons dried oregano

2 teaspoons garlic powder

1 teaspoon kosher salt

½ teaspoon freshly ground black pepper

grilled vegetables

Makes 6 main-course or lunch servings, or 8 to 10 side-dish servings

Here's the most basic recipe for grilled vegetables. Feel free to add your favorites. As an alternative to the Parmigiano-Reggiano and basil finish, offer balsamic vinegar for drizzling over the vegetables.

Extra-virgin olive oil

1 large zucchini, ends trimmed, cut in half lengthwise

1 large yellow summer squash, ends trimmed, cut in half lengthwise

1 large head radicchio, cut into sixths, but leaves left attached at the root end

1 medium fennel bulb, fronds removed, tough bottom trimmed, cut lengthwise into six ⅛- to ¼-inch-thick slices

1 medium eggplant (choose an elongated one), trimmed, cut crosswise into twelve ½-inch-thick rounds

6 medium red-skinned potatoes, scrubbed but unpeeled, cut lengthwise into sixths

Kosher salt

Freshly ground black pepper

About 1 tablespoon extra-virgin olive oil

½ cup chopped fresh basil

½ cup freshly grated Parmigiano-Reggiano cheese

1 Prepare an outdoor grill for direct cooking over medium-high heat (450°F).

2 Toss the vegetables in a very large bowl with about ¼ cup of olive oil until evenly coated. Season with 1 teaspoon salt and ½ teaspoon pepper.

3 Brush the cooking grate clean. Place the vegetables, arranged neatly by type in groups, on the grate. Grill, with the lid closed as much as possible, with the following timings, transferring the vegetables to a platter as they are cooked.

Zucchini and summer squash: Cook until the underside is seared with grill marks, about 3 minutes. Flip and cook until the opposite side is seared, and the zucchini and squash are just tender, about 3 minutes more.

Radicchio: Cook, turning occasionally, until wilted and lightly browned, about 6 minutes.

Fennel: Cook until the underside is seared with grill marks, about 4 minutes. Flip and cook until the opposite side is seared, the edges are browned, and the fennel is crisp-tender, 3 to 5 minutes more.

Eggplant: Cook until the underside is browned, about 4 minutes. Flip and cook until the opposite side is browned and the eggplant is tender, about 4 minutes more.

Potatoes: Be sure the potatoes are facing cut-side down on the grill. Cook until the cut side of the potato facing the heat is golden brown, about 10 minutes. Flip and cook until the opposite side is browned, about 10 minutes more. If the potatoes threaten to burn before they are done, reduce the grill heat. (For a charcoal grill, move them to an area of the grate not directly over the coals.)

4 Cut each zucchini and yellow squash slice in thirds crosswise. (If serving as a side dish, you might want to cut some of the other vegetables into smaller serving pieces, too.) Drizzle the vegetables with about 1 tablespoon of extra-virgin olive oil. Sprinkle with the basil and cheese. Season to taste with salt and pepper and serve warm or at room temperature.

desserts

IT'S EASY TO OVERLOOK COOKING DESSERTS ON THE GRILL. WE ARE all familiar with grilled fruits and a few other goodies, but the possibilities go well beyond them. Consider the fact that your grill can be used as an outdoor oven, and the possibilities become more apparent. Yes, you can bake a cake and make a cobbler outside. Laura Augsburger, a pastry chef at Rao's Caesars Palace, has created this collection of stellar desserts that ranges from easy, make-ahead sweets to ones that show off your grilling prowess.

grilled apples with caramel sauce

Good apples are available year-round, so you can enjoy them whenever you want without waiting for a seasonal appearance. Baked apples are always a delicious way to end a meal. Here they are topped with an oatmeal streusel and grilled in foil packets. Keep your wits about you when making the caramel sauce, as it cooks quickly and needs constant attention.

CARAMEL SAUCE

1 cup granulated sugar

½ teaspoon freshly squeezed lemon juice

⅔ cup heavy cream, warmed

2 tablespoons unsalted butter

APPLES

¼ cup (½ stick) unsalted butter, at room temperature

¼ cup packed light brown sugar

¼ cup rolled (old-fashioned) oats or quick-cooking oatmeal

2 tablespoons coarsely chopped walnuts

2 tablespoons dried raisins or cranberries

⅛ teaspoon ground cinnamon

6 Granny Smith or Golden Delicious apples, cored

Nonstick vegetable oil spray

Vanilla ice cream for serving (optional)

1 Prepare an outdoor grill for direct cooking over medium heat (350°F).

2 **To make the caramel sauce:** Bring the sugar, ¼ cup water, and lemon juice to a boil in a heavy-bottomed medium saucepan, stirring just until the sugar is dissolved. Cook without stirring, occasionally swirling the saucepan by the handle, and brushing down the sugar crystals on the side of the saucepan with a bristle brush dipped in cold water, until the caramel is about the color of a copper penny and smoking, about 3 minutes. Remove from the heat and slowly add the cream, being careful that the sauce doesn't boil over. Add the butter and stir until the sauce is smooth, returning to low heat, if necessary, to dissolve the caramel. Let cool until warm. (The sauce can be cooled, covered, and refrigerated up to 1 day ahead. Reheat over low heat.)

3 **To prepare the apples:** Mix the butter and brown sugar together in a medium bowl with an electric mixer on high speed until the mixture is pale, about 1 minute. Stir in the oatmeal, walnuts, raisins, and cinnamon. Stuff the oatmeal mixture into the cored center of each apple.

4 For each serving, spray the dull side of a 12-inch-square piece of heavy-duty aluminum foil with nonstick vegetable oil. Place a stuffed apple in the center of the foil. Close up the foil, leaving some headroom above the apple.

5 Place the foil packets on the grate. Close the grill lid. Cook until the apples are tender, about 20 minutes. For each serving, carefully open the foil—watch out for steam—and transfer the apple and its juices to a bowl. Drizzle with the caramel sauce and serve warm, with vanilla ice cream if desired.

grilled banana, caramel,
and chocolate chip ice cream

Makes about 1½ quarts

One of the old-fashioned images of summertime was a hand-cranked ice-cream machine on the back porch. Today's ice-cream machines are inexpensive and much easier to use—you will not need crushed ice or rock salt, just an electric outlet. This is one outrageous ice cream, with chunks of grilled bananas, chocolate chips, nuts, and caramel sauce running through it. Mix it up with another sauce (hot fudge, butterscotch, or marshmallow) or even peanut butter instead of the caramel.

ICE CREAM BASE

2 large eggs

½ cup sugar

1 cup half-and-half

1 (5-ounce) can evaporated milk

2 cups heavy cream

1 (3.4-ounce) box vanilla instant pudding

1 tablespoon pure vanilla extract

3 ripe bananas, skin on

1 (12.25-ounce) jar caramel sauce

1 cup semisweet or milk chocolate chips

1 cup (4 ounces) coarsely chopped walnuts, pecans, or almonds (optional)

1 Whisk the eggs and sugar in a heatproof medium bowl until pale. Heat the half-and-half and evaporated milk in a medium saucepan over medium heat until bubbles appear around the liquid's edges. Gradually whisk the hot milk mixture into the eggs, then pour the mixture back into the saucepan. Stirring constantly with a wooden spoon, cook over medium-low heat until an instant-read thermometer inserted in the custard reads 185°F, about 3 minutes. The mixture should be steaming; do not boil. Strain through a fine-mesh sieve into a bowl. Let cool completely. Cover with plastic wrap and refrigerate until chilled, at least 4 hours or overnight.

2 Whisk the heavy cream, pudding, and vanilla together in a large bowl. Whisk in the custard. Pour into your ice-cream maker and churn according to the manufacturer's directions. (You may have to do this in two batches, depending on your machine's capacity.) Transfer the ice cream to an airtight container, cover, and freeze until firmer, but not solid, about 2 hours.

3 Meanwhile, prepare an outdoor grill for direct cooking over medium-high heat (450°F).

4 Brush the cooking grate clean and lightly oil the grate. Cut each banana lengthwise, cutting to, but not through, the skin. Brush the cut sides of each banana with about 2 tablespoons of the caramel sauce. Place on the grate, cut-sides down. Grill until the banana flesh is caramelized, about 2 minutes. Turn the bananas and grill until the skins are blackened, about 1 minute more. Transfer to a plate and cool completely. Peel the bananas and cut into ½-inch chunks.

5 When the ice cream has firmed, gradually stir in the bananas, the remaining caramel sauce, chocolate chips, and walnuts, if using. Return to the container and freeze until firm enough to scoop, at least 4 hours or overnight. Scoop into bowls and serve.

CHOCOLATE GRILLED BANANA ICE CREAM:
Substitute chocolate instant pudding mix for vanilla.

candy bar banana "splits"

Makes 4 servings

We all know how to make a banana split, but this one has warm bananas grilled with your favorite candy bar in foil to make a gooey sauce. This book's editor, Elizabeth Beier, made these for her kids, and the youngsters were fascinated by what she could possibly be doing with their carefully selected candy bars and a live grill. They were thrilled with the results! Go ahead and add ice cream, although these are rich enough without it.

WHIPPED CREAM

½ cup heavy cream

2 teaspoons sugar

½ teaspoon pure vanilla extract

4 bananas

2 of your favorite chocolate-coated candy bars, cut into bite-size pieces

1 cup hot fudge or caramel ice-cream topping, heated

¼ cup chopped pecans, walnuts, or almonds

1 **To make the whipped cream:** Whip the cream, sugar, and vanilla in a chilled medium bowl with an electric mixer, fitted with the wire whisk, on high speed until stiff. Cover and refrigerate until ready to serve.

2 Prepare an outdoor grill for direct cooking over medium-high heat (450°F).

3 Split a banana lengthwise, cutting to, but not through, the skin on the bottom. Open up the banana. Place on a 12-inch square of heavy-duty aluminum foil. Fill the opened banana with one-fourth of the chopped candy bars. Close up the foil, leaving some headroom at the top. Repeat with the remaining bananas and chopped candy bars.

4 Place the bananas on the grill grate. Cook, with the lid closed as much as possible, until the bananas are heated through and the candy bar has melted (open a foil packet to check, but be careful of escaping steam), about 5 minutes.

5 For each serving, carefully unwrap a banana. Using a spoon as an aide, ease the banana, with the clinging melted candy bar "sauce," out of its skin and into a dessert bowl. Add about ¼ cup of ice-cream topping to each. Top with a large dollop of whipped cream and a sprinkle of chopped pecans. Serve immediately.

maple nut granola

I bet you never thought of cooking granola on a grill, but it works like a dream. Granola can go beyond the breakfast table to become a crisp topping for grilled fruit, turning it into a summer crumble. Or take it a step further and layer the granola with fruit and vanilla yogurt for a more substantial dessert.

Makes about 5½ cups

1 Prepare an outdoor grill for indirect cooking over medium heat (350°F). Coat a 13 × 9-inch metal baking pan with the vegetable oil spray.

2 Mix all of the ingredients except the dried cranberries in a large bowl. Spread out in the pan.

3 Place the pan on the side of the grill opposite the heat source. Cook the granola, with the lid closed as much as possible, stirring well every 10 minutes, until the oatmeal is toasted and fragrant, about 30 minutes. Remove from the grill and let cool completely. Stir in the dried cranberries. Use immediately or store in an airtight container at room temperature for up to 2 weeks.

Nonstick vegetable oil spray

3 cups rolled (old-fashioned) oats

½ cup sliced or slivered almonds

½ cup coarsely chopped walnuts

½ cup coarsely chopped pecans

½ cup maple syrup

½ teaspoon kosher salt

½ teaspoon ground cinnamon

¼ teaspoon ground cloves

1 cup dried cranberries or raisins

cherry cobbler

Makes 6 servings

Cherries are a true summertime pleasure, and cherry cobbler is a great way to enjoy them. But it takes a lot of cherries to make a cobbler, so why not start with a can of cherry pie filling? If you want to pit your own cherries, be sure to get a cherry pitter, or just use frozen cherries.

FILLING

2 tablespoons unsalted butter, melted, plus more for the pan

1 (21-ounce) can cherry pie filling

1½ cups pitted fresh Bing or thawed frozen sweet cherries

2 tablespoons sugar

TOPPING

1¼ cups all-purpose flour, plus more for rolling out the biscuits

1¼ teaspoons baking powder

1 tablespoon sugar

½ teaspoon kosher salt

5 tablespoons cold unsalted butter, cut into ½-inch cubes

1 large egg

½ cup buttermilk

Vanilla ice cream for serving

OPTIONAL: If you wish, substitute one 16.3-ounce package Pillsbury Grands! Frozen Buttermilk Biscuits, thawed, for the biscuit topping.

1 Prepare an outdoor grill for indirect cooking over medium-high heat (450°F). Butter an 8-inch-square metal baking pan.

2 **To make the filling:** Combine all of the filling ingredients in a medium bowl. Pour into the baking pan.

3 **To make the topping:** Whisk the flour, baking powder, sugar, and salt together in a mixer bowl. Add the butter and cut in with an electric mixer fitted with the paddle attachment on slow speed until the mixture looks like coarse crumbs with some pea-size pieces of butter. Stir in the egg, then the buttermilk, to make a rough dough. Turn out the dough onto a lightly floured work surface. Gently knead the dough just until it comes together; do not overwork the dough. Pat it out into a ½-inch-thick round. Pull off 9 equal portions of the dough (they shouldn't be perfect) and place on the cherry filling. Cover the pan with aluminum foil.

4 Place the cobbler on the side of the grill opposite the heat source. Cook, with the lid closed as much as possible, for 20 minutes. Remove the foil and cook until the topping is lightly browned and the filling is bubbling, about 5 minutes more. Remove from the grill and let cool for 5 to 10 minutes. Spoon into bowls and serve warm with ice cream.

grilled fruit kebabs
with cream cheese dip

The fruits in the recipe are really just suggestions, so feel free to substitute whatever is ripe and looks good at the market—apricots, plums, nectarines, and pears also do well on the grill. Be sure the grill is well cleaned of any residual flavors from the main course—you don't want garlic on your fruit kebabs.

Makes 6 servings

1 **To make the dipping sauce:** Mash the cream cheese in a medium bowl with a rubber spatula until smooth. Fold in the whipped topping, then gradually fold in the pudding mix. Cover and refrigerate until chilled, at least 1 hour or up to 1 day.

2 Prepare an outdoor grill for direct cooking over medium heat (350°F).

3 On each skewer, spear 3 pineapple chunks, and 2 each of strawberries, mango chunks, and peach chunks. Whisk together the lemon juice, melted butter, and brown sugar in a small bowl to dissolve the brown sugar. Set the lemon glaze aside.

4 Brush the grill grate clean and lightly oil the grate. Place the kebabs, running perpendicular to the grid, on the grate. Brush each kebab with the lemon glaze. Grill, with the lid closed as much as possible, turning and brushing occasionally with more of the lemon glaze, until the fruit is lightly browned, about 5 minutes.

5 Divide the dip among six small bowls. For each serving, slide the fruit off the skewer onto a plate. Add a bowl of dip and serve immediately.

DIPPING SAUCE

8 ounces cream cheese, softened

1 (8-ounce) container thawed frozen whipped dessert topping

1 (3.4-ounce) box instant vanilla pudding mix

6 metal skewers or 6 long bamboo skewers soaked in water for 1 hour, drained

½ ripe pineapple, cored, peeled, and cut into 18 chunks

12 large strawberries, hulled

2 ripe mangoes, pitted, peeled, and cut into 6 chunks each

2 ripe peaches, pitted, cut into 6 chunks each

2 tablespoons freshly squeezed lemon juice

2 tablespoons unsalted butter, melted

2 tablespoons light brown sugar

s'mores bread puddings

Makes 8 servings

The irresistible pairing of marshmallows and chocolate is celebrated in these individual bread puddings. Serve them warm for a satisfying comfort food, right off the grill. If you prefer not to use ramekins, spread the bread mixture in a buttered 9 × 9-inch metal baking dish, and cook on the grill for about 45 minutes, covered with aluminum foil for half of the cooking time.

Butter, for greasing the ramekins

2½ cups whole milk

6 large eggs, lightly beaten

¼ teaspoon pure vanilla extract

⅔ cup sugar

¼ teaspoon ground cinnamon

8 cups (about 12 slices) white bread, cubed

2 cups miniature marshmallows

1½ cups (9 ounces) semisweet chocolate chips

MARSHMALLOW DRIZZLE

½ cup miniature marshmallows

½ cup semisweet chocolate chips

¼ cup whole milk

1 Prepare an outdoor grill for indirect cooking over medium-high heat (450°F). Lightly butter eight 8-ounce ramekins.

2 Whisk the milk, eggs, and vanilla in a large bowl. Mix together the sugar and cinnamon in a small bowl. (This helps the cinnamon from clumping when added to the liquids.) Add the cinnamon-sugar to the egg-milk mixture and whisk. Add the bread cubes, marshmallows, and chocolate chips to the milk mixture and stir well. Let stand for 10 minutes to allow the bread to soak up some of the liquid. Spoon equal amounts of the pudding into the ramekins. Cover each ramekin loosely with aluminum foil.

3 Place the ramekins on the cooler side of the grill, not over the heat source. Cook, with the lid closed as much as possible, for 10 minutes. Remove the foil and continue cooking until the puddings are puffed and golden brown and a knife inserted in the center of a pudding comes out clean, about 10 minutes more. Remove the ramekins from the grill.

4 **To make the marshmallow drizzle:** Combine the marshmallows, chocolate chips, and milk together in a small saucepan over low heat. Cook, stirring often, until melted and smooth, about 5 minutes. Drizzle some of the marshmallow mixture over each pudding and serve warm.

laura's grilled pound cake
with mixed berries

This is one of the easiest of all summer desserts. With fresh seasonal berries as the star attraction, it never fails to please, and topped with a dollop of white whipped cream, it has all of the colors and elements of a Fourth of July treat. Make the compote a few hours before serving so the berries can give off some juices.

Makes 6 servings

1 **To make the berry compote:** Bring the sugar and ½ cup water to a boil in a small saucepan over high heat, stirring to dissolve the sugar. Let the syrup cool. Combine the raspberries, blueberries, blackberries, and strawberries and stir in enough of the syrup to sweeten the berries to taste. Cover and refrigerate for at least 2 hours and up to 8 hours.

2 Prepare an outdoor grill for direct cooking over medium heat (350°F).

3 Brush the cooking grate clean and lightly oil the grate. Spread the butter over both sides of the pound cake slices. Place the cake slices on the grill. Cook, turning once, until lightly browned on both sides, about 4 minutes.

4 For each serving, place a cake slice on a plate and top with the berries and their juices. Add a dollop of whipped cream, if desired. Serve immediately.

BERRY COMPOTE

½ cup sugar

1 (6-ounce) basket fresh raspberries

1 (6-ounce) basket fresh blueberries

1 (6-ounce) basket fresh blackberries

1 pint fresh strawberries, hulled and quartered

3 tablespoons unsalted butter, well softened

1 store-bought pound cake, cut into six 1½-inch slices

Whipped cream (see step 1, page 140) for serving (optional)

laura's mini dessert pizza

Makes 9 servings

The fun part about this easy dessert is that you can use your favorite ingredients to personalize the pizza. Like chocolate chip dough better than sugar dough? Go ahead and use it. Or go all peanut with peanut cookie dough, peanut butter, and peanut chips.

1 (16.5-ounce) package of your favorite refrigerated cookie dough

1 (13-ounce) chocolate hazelnut spread, such as Nutella, or peanut butter, or almond butter, warmed

1 cup semisweet or milk chocolate chips

1 cup white chocolate, peanut butter, or butterscotch chips

½ cup coarsely chopped walnuts or peanuts (optional)

½ cup miniature marshmallows (optional)

1 Preheat an outdoor grill for indirect cooking with medium heat (350°F).

2 Break apart the cookie dough and place it on an ungreased 13 x 9-inch metal baking pan, pressing the dough into the pan until it fills the pan in an even layer. If you have a large gas grill, you can use a 12- to 14-inch diameter nonperforated pizza pan.

3 Place the pan on the unheated side of the grill. Cook, with the lid closed as much as possible, rotating the pan if needed for even cooking (the side nearest the heat source will cook more quickly) until the cookie dough is lightly browned, about 10 minutes. Remove the pan from the grill and let cool slightly.

4 Spread the chocolate hazelnut spread over each cookie. Sprinkle the semisweet and white chocolate chips, adding the walnuts or marshmallows, if using. Return the pan to the grill, reduce flame to low, and continue cooking until the chips melt, about 4 minutes. Remove from the grill. Let cool, cut, and serve.

pineapple upside-down cake

When I noticed a resurgence of pineapple upside-down cake on restaurant menus, I decided to try it on the grill. Chef Laura created this easy version using cake mix, with the brilliant touch of replacing the liquid in the package directions with coconut milk, a trick that adds rich sweetness and density to the cake.

Makes 9 to 12 servings

1 Prepare an outdoor grill for direct and indirect grilling over medium heat (350°F). Lightly butter a 13 × 9-inch metal baking pan.

2 Brush the cooking grate clean and lightly oil the grate. Lightly brush the pineapple rings with 2 tablespoons of melted butter. Place the pineapple rings on the hot side of the grill. Cook until seared with grill marks on both sides, about 3 minutes. Transfer to a plate.

3 Combine the remaining 4 tablespoons of melted butter and brown sugar in the baking pan. Place over the heat source on the grill. Cook until the brown sugar melts, about 2 minutes, stirring occasionally. Pour into the pan. Arrange the pineapple slices on top, and place a cherry in the center of each slice.

4 Make the cake according to the package directions, substituting coconut milk for the water. Spread the batter in the pan.

5 Place on the cool side of the grill. Cover and grill, with the lid closed as much as possible, until the cake springs back when pressed in the center with a fingertip, about 35 minutes. Let cool on a wire cake rack for 10 minutes.

6 Run a knife around the inside of the pan to loosen the cake. Invert and unmold the cake onto an oblong platter. If the pineapple sticks to the pan, just pry it off and replace it on the cake. Slice and serve.

1 (20-ounce) can pineapple rings in juice, drained, or fresh, peeled, cored, and diced

6 tablespoons (¾ stick) unsalted butter, melted

1 cup packed brown sugar

10 fresh pitted Bing or maraschino cherries

1 (18.25-ounce) box pineapple supreme cake mix

Unsweetened coconut milk (well shaken), as needed

Vegetable oil, as needed

Large eggs, as needed

grilled peaches
with mascarpone mousse

Makes 6 servings

Mascarpone is so buttery and rich, it doesn't take much to turn it into a dessert. Here it is given a mousse-like texture with whipped cream, and served over tender, juicy peaches. Use either domestic or imported Italian mascarpone—they're both good.

BASTING MIXTURE

2 tablespoons unsalted butter

2 tablespoons freshly squeezed lemon juice

2 tablespoons light brown sugar

Dash of ground cinnamon

MASCARPONE MOUSSE

½ cup heavy cream

1 tablespoon confectioners' sugar

3 tablespoons honey, plus more to taste

1 cup mascarpone cheese

1 vanilla bean, split lengthwise

6 ripe peaches, halved lengthwise and pitted

¼ cup toasted and coarsely chopped walnuts (see Note)

6 mint sprigs

1 **To make the basting mixture:** Melt the butter in a small saucepan over low heat (or melt in a small bowl in a microwave). Add the lemon juice. Stir in the brown sugar and cinnamon. (If the mixture cools and sets, reheat briefly until pourable.)

2 **To make the mascarpone mousse:** Whip the heavy cream, confectioners' sugar, and 1 tablespoon of honey in a chilled mixer bowl with an electric mixer fitted with the wire whisk on high speed until stiff. Put the mascarpone in another bowl. Using the tip of a small sharp knife, scrape the seeds from the vanilla bean into the mascarpone. Add the remaining 2 tablespoons honey and mash with a rubber spatula until combined. Add more honey for a stronger honey flavor, if you wish. Fold in the whipped cream mixture. Cover and refrigerate until ready to serve, up to 6 hours.

3 Prepare an outdoor grill for direct cooking over medium heat (350°F).

4 Brush the cooking grate clean and lightly oil the grate. Brush the peaches with some of the basting mixture. Place the peaches on the cooking grate, cut-side down. Cook, with the lid closed as much as possible, until the peaches are seared with grill marks, about 3 minutes. Turn, brush well with the basting mixture, and grill until the peaches are tender and beginning to brown, 2 to 3 minutes more. Remove from the grill.

5 For each serving, place 2 peach halves in each bowl and top with equal amounts of the mousse and a sprinkle of walnuts. Add a mint sprig and serve immediately.

NOTE: To toast the walnuts, spread on a baking sheet and bake in a preheated 350°F oven, stirring occasionally, until fragrant and light brown, about 10 minutes. Let cool.

acknowledgments

It is imperative that I acknowledge and give thanks to Ed Breslin and to my father, Frank Pellegrino, Sr. When this book was just an idea and in its initial phase of a proposal, both gentlemen not only encouraged me to move forward with this project but provided great support, insight, and motivation. I must also acknowledge and thank Elizabeth Beier, Michelle Richter, and their team at St. Martin's Press for giving this book the green light, but also for their tremendous support and creativity. I also thank Elizabeth for introducing me to, and affording me the opportunity to work with, the ever great and accomplished food writer, Rick Rodgers.

I especially thank my dear friend Grace Bascos for embarking upon this journey with me. She is not only a superb writer, but a dear friend and colleague in the food world.

I honor our family's restaurant, Rao's. Heaven only knows where I'd be without the birth of this institution 115 years ago. The history, our team, and our guests for the last quarter century have truly formed me. I will be forever grateful for the love and tutelage my grand aunt Anna and grand uncle Vincent imparted to me and only hope to keep their vision alive for the next century and make them proud.

I also extend a big thanks to Ron Straci, my cousin and partner, with whom I've had the pleasure to work for over twenty years. I am especially appreciative of his support and advice over the past decade.

Josephine Pellegrino, my mother, has always been terrific to me and I can never thank her enough for her unconditional love and support.

A special salute to my culinary team and managers in New York and Las Vegas: Joey, Patrick, Sergio, and MJ. These young emerging superstars have been vital to our current success and I look forward to working with them in the future. To Chef Dino, Chef Nicole, Chef Fatimah, and Chef Laura: Thank you!! A special thanks to Caesar's Palace and the executive team there.

To my daughters Annie and Marcelle, you both have enriched my life and provided me with the opportunity to experience love on another level. I hope this book provides you both with the knowledge that you can achieve anything you set out to do.

Finally, a special thanks to my dear friend, Henry Marks, for helping me to keep focused; his sage words and advice were always there when needed.

index